DATE DUE			

77623
Holzer

St. Procopius College Library

Maple Ave. and College Rd.

Lisle, Illinois

PSYCHIC INVESTIGATOR

OTHER BOOKS BY HANS HOLZER

Predictions: Fact or Fallacy?
ESP and You
The Lively Ghosts of Ireland
Yankee Ghosts
Ghosts I've Met
Ghost Hunter

PSYCHIC INVESTIGATOR

HANS HOLZER

HAWTHORN BOOKS, INC., NEW YORK

W. Clement Stone, Publisher

St. Procopius College Library
Lisle, Illinois 60532

133.1
H74p

Copyright © 1968 by Hans Holzer.

Copyright under International and Pan-American Copyright Conventions. All rights reserved, including the right to reproduce this book, or portions thereof, in any form, except for the inclusion of brief quotations in a review. All inquiries should be addressed to Hawthorn Books, Inc., 70 Fifth Avenue, New York City 10011. This book was manufactured in the United States of America and published simultaneously in Canada by Prentice-Hall of Canada, Ltd., 1870 Birchmount Road, Scarborough, Ontario. Library of Congress Catalogue Card Number: 68-30711.

Designed by Gene Gordon

First Edition: 1968

Second Printing: 1968

77623

CONTENTS

PSYCHIC INVESTIGATOR

1

THE PSYCHIC WORLD

"Enough of this nonsense," the kindergarten teacher, Miss Seidler, said sternly, and a hush fell upon the assembled children. There were seven or eight boys and girls, roughly three or four years old, grouped around a boy of three who sat on a wooden chair in the middle of an imperfect circle. Imperfect was right. Teacher did not approve of our activities. The little boy in the middle was I, and I had been telling the kids some of the wildest ghost stories ever heard anywhere since Edgar Allan Poe was in knee pants.

Tales of the supernatural seemed to come to me easily, as if I had been born to tell them; where I got my raw materials is still a mystery to me. But apparently the plots hit home, parents started to complain that their offspring wouldn't sleep nights, demanding more and better ghost stories, and what the heck were they teaching their youngsters at Miss Seidler's?

It was clear that Miss Seidler did not intend to make ghost-story telling a regular—or even an irregular—part of the curriculum.

"Hans," she now demanded, "let me see that."

"That" was the book of wisdom I had been holding in my hands, pretending to read from it. It was a little futuristic, for I could neither read nor write at that point, but I had seen grownups doing it, so I copied the custom. My book was no ordinary book, however. It was my father's trolley car pass, expired, in a nice, black leather cover. Miss Seidler was not impressed.

After a moment of silence, she returned the *legitimation*, the pass, to me and told me to stop telling ghost stories.

But you can't keep a good man down. By the time I was six, I was regaling my mother's family in Moravia with tales told me, allegedly, by the wood sprites in the trees along the little river that flows through the city of Bruenn, where I spent every summer during those years. My beginnings in the psychic field were humble, to say the least, and about as far from factuality as you can go.

Fortunately my uncle Henry was a dreamer and understanding. At his side, I had my first whiff of the real thing: psychic experiences really existed, I was informed, and my interest was now doubly aroused. Uncle Henry of course did not treat me like a parapsychologist: I was a boy of maybe nine or ten and I liked adventure, and that was precisely what he was going to give me. In his room, furnished exclusively with eighteenth-century furniture and antiques, we held seances in candlelight. He had some early books dealing with the occult, and used to read from them the way a minister interprets the Bible. Since most of it was in distorted Latin, the sound but not the meaning penetrated my consciousness, and it was all very exciting.

Uncle Henry did not say there were ghosts and spirits; neither did he say there weren't. It was all I needed to have my secret work cut out for me; a responsible adult approved, so I was doing the right thing!

As the years passed, my interests veered toward science and the unconquered territories of electronics and radio. A new rationalism grew in my mind and I became very cocky in my attitude toward anything I could not touch, see, hear, or feel at this point: how *could* such things as spirits exist?

There had to be a "natural" explanation, regardless of the evidence presented! I was completely unwilling to regard an unseen world around us as anything but pure fantasy, remnant of childhood memories, and totally incompatible with my brave new world of electronics.

I was about ten at the time and such silly attitudes were perhaps normal for my age. But I know some mature, intelligent adults who have exactly the same sort of reasoning. There is that television producer, for instance, who patiently listened to all the evidence for the existence of psychic phenomena, looked carefully at the photographs taken under test conditions, and even managed to have an experience with strange pictures himself—to no avail.

"There's got to be some other explanation," he would intone regularly. He, like many others in our materialistic world today, is incapable of accepting the truth unless that truth conforms to his preconceived notions as to what that truth must look like. It is a little like the bed of Procrustes. Procrustes, you may recall, was a highwayman in ancient Greece whose particular brand of fun consisted of placing unwary travelers into his "special" bed: if they were too long, he'd cut them down, if they were too short, he'd stretch them to fit.

I did not attend the ordinary, tuition-free high school in my ancestral city of Vienna, Austria, but managed to get into a *Gymnasium*, a combination of high school and junior college, with emphasis on the humanities. My electronics spirit had somehow departed along the way, and was now replaced by a burning desire to become an archaeologist. Children often change their plans dozens of times during their school days, depending on what influences them in the world around them. But in my case, at least, the label stuck, and I did indeed become an archaeologist—at least at first.

This was in the 1930s, when Europe seethed with political

unrest and the madman of Berlin already cast a heavy shadow upon smaller countries around Germany such as the Austria I grew up in. It seemed foolish, on the face of it, to study history and the humanities in *Gymnasium* in order to continue at the university in the hopes of eventually becoming an archaeologist, at a time when more practical pursuits might have been wiser. I also evinced a strong interest in writing, and it was clear to me that I would be a *Schriftsteller*—an author—of some kind, exactly what I have become, of course. But in the 1930s, when I was in my early teens, this was really quite outlandish to my parents and friends.

In the second half of my *Gymnasium* period, when I was sixteen years old, I was profoundly impressed by one of my teachers, Franz Spunda. This of course brought me into immediate disrepute with most of my classmates since Dr. Spunda was one of the least-liked teachers and one of the most feared.

The reasons for this were in the man's character: he was a taciturn, dour man who seldom joked or said an unnecessary word and whose scholastic behavior was stern and uncompromising. Other teachers you could soften up, but not him. What impressed me about Franz Spunda, however, was not the fact that he was disliked by my classmates, of course, for I am not a nonconformist for its own sake. Spunda was a well-known writer of historical novels and, like so many authors, even successful ones, was forced to augment his income by teaching.

Perhaps he resented this, for it interfered with his more important work, but his storehouse of knowledge was greater than called for in his teaching position. His classes dealt with literature, as was to be expected, but I soon discovered that Dr. Spunda had a deep interest in the occult, just as I used to have in the old Uncle Henry days.

I read some of Spunda's books, which led to other books

on occult subjects, notably the very technical books on parapsychology by Professor Oesterreicher and by G. W. Gessmann, both published in the 1920s, and acquired by me in 1935 when I was fifteen. Suddenly I realized that there was truth in these accounts and that it was worthy of my further efforts to involve myself in the study of the occult. Whenever I had an opportunity, I let Dr. Spunda know that I shared his interests in these fields. On one occasion I picked as the topic for a paper the rather cumbersome title of "Dr. von Schrenck-Notzing's Theory of the Telekinetic, Teleplastic Ideoplasticity," and confounded my classmates by just the title, to say nothing of the contents!

But not Dr. Spunda. After I was through reading my paper, he remarked that it was a hodgepodge of several theories and proceeded to criticize my statements with the experienced approach of an inside man. After that, it became clear to my classmates that I was something special, and many avoided me afterward in anything but the most mundane relationships. It suited me fine, for I preferred a few close friends to general and shallow popularity.

Many years later, when I returned to Vienna as an American foreign correspondent, I met my erstwhile teacher again in the stillness of his cottage in the suburbs of Vienna. We talked freely of the past and he admitted his errors of a political nature: Spunda had welcomed the Hitler movement at first with the unrealistic emotional optimism of a Wagnerian revivalist of Pan-Germanic days, only to find the bitter truth difficult to accept. Essentially a religious man, he realized in the later war years that the German cause had been betrayed by the Third Reich, but he had a difficult time cleansing himself of his association with it for many years after. And yet, he had never done anything overt, and never denied his mistakes. Eventually his books were published again and some are still in print, especially his very profound work on the rose cross, *Jacob Boehme*, which Bauer republished recently. Spunda has since gone on in a manner worthy of his Olympian philosophy: he died of a heart attack during a trip exploring once again the beauty of ancient Greece.

At the University of Vienna, my days were occupied with the formal studies of archaeology and history, and psychic matters had to wait. In 1938 we decided that the threatening war clouds would soon erupt into rainstorms of blood and destruction, and I went to live in New York, where my father had spent many years at the turn of the century as an immigrant. All this time, my interest in the world of the sixth sense lay dormant, though far from dead. In 1946 I met for the first time Eileen Garrett, whose work has influenced my thinking profoundly even though we do not always agree on the conclusions to be drawn from it.

I was making a reasonably good living as a writer and associate editor of a magazine called *Numismatic Review*, a position utilizing my knowledge of archaeology and ancient numismatics but none of my ESP talents.

The latter grew quietly in the dark, like mushrooms in a tunnel, until suddenly there was need to display them.

I have always maintained that people form links in chains of destiny, each of us furnishing a vital step forward in a journey someone else may be taking without our knowledge where it may lead him. This is our duty then, to serve so that someone else might prosper or succeed, and in turn be served on some other occasion by others in the same manner. Thus it was that the British actor, writer, and comedian Michael Bentine touched off a new wave of psychic interest within me when we met in London in 1950, backstage at the Hippodrome Theatre where he was then starring.

Our friendship blossomed particularly when we discovered our common interest in psychic research. When Michael came to New York the following year, we met again.

It so happened that I had also become friendly with the

late Danton Walker, who was for many years the Broadway columnist of the New York *Daily News* and, as I discovered, psychic and very much interested in my favorite subject.

Somehow the link who was Michael Bentine led to the next link, who was Walker, when Walker asked me to arrange an interview with the British star. Now there were three of us, meeting over a drink in Manhattan. During that afternoon, Walker started to tell us of his haunted house in the country and Michael immediately offered to go there with him. But his commitments called him back to England before this could be arranged, and it was I alone who went —with the famous medium Eileen Garrett as "telephone between worlds," using the James Crenshaw description of this gift, and the services of Dr. Robert Laidlaw as observer and arbiter of the investigation that followed.

I have, of course, reported this remarkable case in my earlier book, *Ghost Hunter,* and it has always stood out in my mind as one of the most interesting cases of a haunting I have ever witnessed—and I have had several thousand cases since. I don't know whether it was the stark tragedy of a Colonial runner being clubbed to death by the British soldiery and its vivid re-enactment in trance by the medium, or the quality of the witnesses who had experienced the uncanny phenomena I came to know over and over again in the years that followed, but the Rockland County Ghost helped convince me that man does indeed have an immortal component. What this component was began to occupy my time more and more after this case.

Still, I knew only that sometimes things in life go wrong and someone dies tragically and something or other stays behind and becomes a "ghost" of the event. Was it the exception from the norm, and did we usually leave no residue upon expiring? That question occupied my mind a great deal. It seemed entirely consistent with my knowledge of electronics to postulate that man's emotional tensions might constitute an electromagnetic field, similar to a radiation field in the atmosphere. Could it be that these ghosts were really impressions like photographs, in the "ether" or atmosphere of old houses, and did they have no relationship to living human beings. That too seemed vaguely possible under my set of rules. After all, if an atomic explosion can make a part of the atmosphere radioactive for many years, why not a miniature outburst such as sudden death?

At this point in my studies, I was still trying to find some "natural" way of explaining the phenomena I had witnessed, to correlate them with the known facts of science and nature, even though they might be new aspects or little-known facts within the customary framework of human knowledge and understanding. But the Rockland case threw me for a loop: for all intents and purposes, this was not a shallow impression of a past event, but a seemingly living human being from the past, temporarily using the body of the medium, to act out his problems. I could not reconcile what I observed with the concept of a "dead" impression left behind in the atmosphere, and devoid of all further life, all power to react to those making a fresh contact with it. I began to get uncomfortable as I realized what I was trying to do: select my evidence not on the basis of truth but to make the facts fit the theory. Fortunately, I am a very honest fellow. I can't live with half-truths and I don't fool myself about anything when I know, deep within me, that it is wrong.

Consequently, it began to dawn on me that there were psychic cases involving lifeless "impressions" in the atmosphere and then there were cases of authentic hauntings, where a human being was continually reliving his emotional tragedy of the past.

The search was on, for me, for the proof of personal survival, that is to say, evidence of scientific quality that man does survive physical death and continues his existence as a full individual in another dimension.

I realized that ghosts were not exactly ideal cases to prove or disprove the nature of that "other side" of the universe. It had become clear to me that all ghosts were psychotic or at least psychologically disoriented minds and not balanced individuals who had passed on. Obviously, if survival of personality was a fact, it would be far more common than hauntings and the evidence for it should be capable of verification on a much larger scale. More people die "normally" than under tragic conditions, and even among the latter class, those turning up as "ghosts" are again a small portion of the total thus "qualified."

Where was I to turn to find evidence for this so-called spirit world about which the Spiritualists had been talking so nicely for so long, without ever convincing me of its reality?

As for so many others raised in the upper middle class, all emotional religions were alien to my way of life. I grew up considering spiritualist mediums as either outright fakes or at best misguided self-styled prophets and the practice of seances in questionable taste. Should I now reverse myself and seek out some medium and try my hand at a seance, just so I could discover for myself what went on in them? This was not easy, for I hated the dark and wouldn't for the world sit in total darkness.

Torn between letting the matter rest and an aroused curiosity, I attended a number of spiritualist lectures, the kind that attracts a rather motley crowd ranging from frustrated old maids of both sexes to earnest seekers of truth, students of the occult, or just plainly curious people more in need of a fortuneteller than a medium.

On one such occasion I was approached by a man in the crowd, just as the meeting broke up. He explained to me that he had some mediumistic talents which he wished to improve upon, and was therefore trying to arrange a little group to "sit" with him. He hastened to explain also that he was a clerk in Brooklyn and no money was involved in this project. I saw nothing wrong with it and gladly agreed to join him and some others in at least one such meeting. As it happened, they needed a quiet place to meet in, so I suggested my offices on Fifty-ninth Street, New York, after business hours.

That was agreeable, and six ladies whom I had never seen before came up to my office the following evening. They looked like typical New York housewives in their forties and fifties, which is what they were, of course. I pulled down the shades and the gentleman I had met the night before seated himself in one of the chairs and closed his eyes. For a few moments, we were all very quiet and the traffic rumbling by downstairs was all one could hear. Then his breathing became a bit labored and his head fell upon his shoulder.

Rapidly he kept calling out names and bits of information about people that evidently were recognized by one or the other person in the room. Of course I immediately suspected that this was due to his knowing these ladies and trying to please them by "bringing in" their favorite deceased relative. After the seance I questioned them separately and satisfied myself that they had only met him the night before, same as I, at the lecture hall. Evidently my observation that night had not been as good as it should have been, since I did not recall them as being there, but it had been a rather large crowd.

After the fourth or fifth person speaking through the medium, his head turned in my direction and in a voice resembling his normal speaking voice, but somehow strangely distorted, he addressed me now.

"Someone here who knows you . . . named Eric . . . says he died short time ago . . . bad accident . . . wants you to tell loved ones he's all right . . ."

That was all.

But it was enough for me. Half a year before this seance,

a friend of mine had died tragically in an accident while still quite young. His wife had been completely inconsolable since, taking the death of her husband of a few months very hard. His name was Eric.

Of all the people I knew who had passed away in my family not one of them had evidently decided to speak through this medium. But there was certainly something urgent about the message from Eric. His wife needed this bit of news.

I called her and told her, and though she did not really believe in the possibility of personal survival, she was not entirely sure that it didn't exist. An indication that it was possible was all that was needed to help her get over the tragedy gradually, and so she did.

In 1953 I got to know a group that met regularly at the New York headquarters of the Association for Research and Enlightenment, better known as the Edgar Cayce Foundation. This was a study group, and mediums worked with them to learn more about their own abilities. One such budding medium was Ethel Johnson Meyers, who has since become one of our more famous psychics and one of the people I frequently work with in my investigations.

At that time, however, she was just a singing teacher with mediumship who wanted to find out more about herself.

At that time, Ethel's controls—spirit personalities operating her psychic channels to regulate the flow of information and to keep out intruders—were her late husband Albert and a Tibetan named Toto Himalaya. I must confess that Toto sounded absolutely phony to me, somewhat like a vaudeville Indian making grunting noises and behaving very much like a synthetic Tibetan, or one manufactured by the unconscious of the medium herself. This, of course, is an age-old question: are these "controls" real people or are they parts of the personality of the medium and act out consciously in trance that which the medium cannot act out when awake?

I have never been able to prove satisfactorily the objective reality of these controls and some trance mediums, like Sybil Leek, don't even have them. But I haven't any evidence to say that they are anything except what they claim to be, and am of late persuaded to accept them as indeed real human beings who have crossed the threshold into the nonphysical world. Even so great a medium and human being as Eileen Garrett has not been able to make up her own mind on this difficult question.

When I first met Toto via the entranced Ethel Meyers, we had our difficulties, for I don't take kindly to generalities and bits of philosophy that seem to waste both a medium's and an investigator's time.

But if Toto was indeed an ancient Tibetan priest, he had a right to preach. I just wasn't particularly ready to listen to the sermon at that point. Instead, I decided to test Ethel's psychometry talents. Psychometry is the gift of touching an object and describing instantly its history or owners. Naturally, the medium must not know anything about the object or see its shape or outline, to avoid any conscious clues as to its identity.

Consequently, I took the object I had in mind, wrapped it several times in paper and then in pieces of cloth until it became a shapeless parcel of about an arm's length and weighing perhaps three pounds. With this thing under my arm, I came down to the Association where Ethel Meyers was already in the midst of psychometrizing objects. At the first free moment, I thrust the parcel into her outstretched hands and watched for her reactions.

For a moment Mrs. Meyers sat as if stunned. Then, with a shriek, she rose from her chair, at the same time throwing the parcel onto the floor as if I had handed her a burning stick of dynamite.

Even though it was early spring, she was sweating and I could tell she was upset.

"I see a sacrifice," she mumbled, and shuddered.

"This is some kind of ceremony . . . a dagger . . . don't like it." She looked at me sternly, almost reproachfully.

"It's all right, Ethel," I said, "I shan't ask you to touch it again."

With that, I picked up the package and started to unravel it. The others present had formed a circle around us as layer upon layer of cloth and then paper disappeared. Eventually I held in my hand a gleaming *dorje* or Tibetan sacrificial scepter, at the end of which was a dagger. I had meant to make Toto Himalaya feel at home, and all I had succeeded in doing was getting Mrs. Meyers upset!

The following year, after attending dozens upon dozens of meetings at the Association, I made a special visit because my friends had told me of a new medium that had recently joined the experimental group and seemed interesting. I was late in arriving and took a seat in the rear of the already darkened room. At the far end, a woman sat with her eyes closed, while a small red light burned next to her, casting an eerie glow over the assembled people.

This went on for about fifteen minutes—utter silence while the medium slept. Then she awoke and gave messages to some of those present. It was her brand of mediumship, this going out "alone," then returning and talking. Most mediums go into trance and talk during, not after, the trance state. The lights came on now, and I arose to leave. I had walked down the corridor part of the way when the medium I had just observed came after me and stopped me.

"Are you Hans Holzer?"

I nodded, sure someone had told her my name. But nobody had, as I discovered later.

"Then I have a message for you. From an uncle."

Now I have lots of uncles, some dead, some living, and I was not impressed. I looked at her blankly.

The dark-haired woman shook her head impatiently.

"His initials are O. S." she said rapidly, "and he's got a wife named Alice. She's a blonde."

All at once I felt shivers down my spine.

Many years before, an uncle of mine named Otto Stransky had died tragically. I was not particularly close to him, and had not thought of him for years. There had been no reason to do so; his family lived thousands of miles away, in South America, and there was almost no contact.

Whatever it was, the medium certainly had not read my unconscious mind.

His wife's name was indeed Alice. When he lived with her, she was a blonde. At the time of this utterance, however, Alice's hair had long since turned white. Yet, to the timeless memory of her loving husband, the hair would forever be blonde!

That was the first time I had come in contact with a clear-cut message from a departed relative or friend that could not be explained by fraud, coincidence, mind reading or some otherwise explainable cause. It had to be survival of human personality. I thanked the lady, not realizing, at the time, that she would also play a large role in my future work. She is probably one of the finest clairvoyant mediums in America today. Her name is Betty Ritter.

Now I knew that in some instances, at least, proof of survival could be gotten. Then why not in all? Why not indeed. My mind was made up to turn my attention to this end. To give the average person the facts of afterlife, in terms he can both understand and accept; to be a scientist but not a negative doubter. Truth does not need interpretation, just exposure.

That's how I became the Psychic Investigator I still am today.

2

THE HAUNTED TRAILER

Sometimes, one would think, the work of a Psychic Investigator must be downright drab. Little old ladies having nightmares, imaginative teenagers letting off steam over frustrations in directions as yet unexplored, neurotics of uncertain sex fantasizing about their special roles and talents. All this is grist for the investigator's mill, poor chap, and he has to listen and nod politely, for that's how he gets information. (As when Peter Lorre whispered across the screen, "Where is the information?" this question is the beacon onto which the psychic sleuth must be drawn.)

And in fact it is perfectly possible for such people to have genuine ESP experiences. Anybody can play this game. All he's got to be is alive and kicking. ESP comes to just about everyone, and there's nothing one can do about it one way or the other.

It is therefore necessary to have a completely open mind as to the kind of individual who might have a psychic experience of validity. I can attest to this need to my regret. Several years ago, people approached me who had witnessed the amazing Ted Serios demonstrate his thought photography and who wanted me to work with the fellow. But my quasi-middle-class sense of propriety shied away from the midwestern bellhop when I realized that he drank and was not altogether of drawing-room class. How wrong I was! A little later, Professor Jule Eisenbud of the University of Colorado showed better sense and less prejudice as to a person's private habits, and his work with Serios is not only a scientific breakthrough of the first order, but was turned into a successful book for Eisenbud as well.

Of course I don't expect my subjects to be proprietors of New England mansions about to collapse, or Southern plantation owners drinking mint juleps on their lawns, but I have yet to hear from a truck driver who has seen a ghost, or a State Department man with premonitions. Hindsight maybe, but not precognition.

So it was with more than casual interest that I received a communication (via the U.S. mail) from a comely young lady named Rita Atlanta. That she was indeed comely I found out later from her Christmas cards. Christmas cards don't hardly come any comelier. Hers show all of Rita in a champagne glass (a very large champagne glass without champagne in it—only Rita) underneath a Christmas tree, which is very thoughtful of her since she could have been placed into a Christmas stocking and what a shame that would have been, at least in part.

Her initial letter, however, had no such goodies in it, but merely requested that I help her get rid of her ghost. Such requests are of course not unusual, but this one was—and I am not referring to the lady's occupation, which was that of an exotic dancer in sundry nightclubs aroud the more or less civilized world.

What made her case unusual was the fact that "her" ghost appeared in a thirty-year-old trailer near Boston.

"When I told my husband that we had a ghost," she wrote, "he laughed and said, 'Why should a respectable ghost move into a trailer? We have hardly room in it ourselves with three kids.' "

It seemed the whole business had started in the summer

of 1964 when the specter made its first, sudden appearance. Although her husband could not see what she saw, Miss Atlanta's pet skunk evidently didn't like it and moved into another room. Three months later, her husband passed away, and Miss Atlanta was kept busy hopping the Atlantic (hence her stage name) in quest of nightclub work.

Ever since her first encounter with the figure of a man in her Massachusetts trailer, the dancer had kept the lights burning all night long. As someone once put it, "I don't believe in ghosts, but I'm scared of them."

Despite the lights, Miss Atlanta always felt a presence at the same time her initial experience had taken place—between three and three-thirty in the morning. It would awaken her with such a regularity that at last she decided to seek help.

At the time she contacted me she was appearing nightly at the Imperial in Frankfurt, taking a bath onstage in an oversize champagne glass with under-quality champagne. The discriminating clientele that frequents the Imperial of course loved the French touch, and Rita Atlanta was and is a wow.

I discovered that her late husband was Colonel Frank Bane, an Air Force ace, who had originally encouraged the Vienna-born girl to change from ballet dancer to belly dancer and eventually to what is termed "exotic" dancing, but which is better described as stripping.

(Not that there is anything wrong with it *per se*, although the Air Force never felt cool under the collar about the whole thing. But the Colonel was a good officer and the boys thought the Colonel's Missus was a good sport—so nobody did anything about it.)

I decided to talk to the "Champagne Bubble Girl" on my next overseas trip, which was in August of 1965. She was working at that time in Stuttgart, but she came over to meet us at our Frankfurt Hotel, and my wife was immediately taken with her pleasant charm, her lack of "show business" phonyness. Then it was discovered that Rita was a Libra, like Catherine, and we repaired for lunch to the terrace of a nearby restaurant to discuss the ups and downs of a hectic life in a champagne glass, not forgetting three kids in a house trailer.

I asked Rita to go through an oriental dance for my camera (minus champagne glass, but not minus anything else) and then we sat down to discuss the ghostly business in earnest. In September of 1963 she and her family had moved into a brand-new trailer in Peabody, Massachusetts. After her encounter with the ghost, Rita made some inquiries about the nice, grassy spot she had chosen to set down the trailer as her home. Nothing had ever stood on the spot before. No ghost stories. Nothing. Just one little thing.

One of the neighbors in the trailer camp, which is at the outskirts of greater Boston, came to see her one evening. By this time Rita's heart was already filled with fear, fear of the unknown that had suddenly come into her life here. She freely confided in her neighbor, a girl by the name of Birdie Gleason.

To her amazement, the neighbor nodded with understanding. She, too, had felt "something," an unseen presence, in her house trailer next to Rita's.

"Sometimes I feel someone is touching me," she added.

"What exactly did *you* see?" I interjected, while outside the street noises of Frankfurt belied the terrifying subject we were discussing.

"I saw a big man, almost seven foot tall, about three hundred to three hundred fifty pounds, and he wore a long coat and a big hat."

But the ghost didn't just stand there glaring at her. Sometimes he made himself comfortable on her kitchen counter. With his ghostly legs dangling down from it. He was as solid as a man of flesh and blood, except that she could not see his face clearly since it was in the darkness of early morning.

Later, when I visited the house trailer with my highly sensitive camera, I took some pictures in the areas indicated by Miss Atlanta—the bedroom, the door to it, and the kitchen counter. In all three areas, strange phenomena manifested on my film. Some mirrorlike transparencies developed in normally opaque areas, which could not and cannot be explained by ordinary facts.

When it happened the first time, she raced for the light, turned the switch, her heart beating in her mouth. The yellowish light of the electric lamp bathed the bedroom in a nightmarish twilight. But the spook had vanished. There was no possible way a real intruder could have come and gone so fast. No way out, no way in. Because this was during the time Boston was being terrorized by the infamous Boston Strangler, Rita had taken special care to double-lock the doors and secure all windows. Nobody could have entered the trailer without making a great deal of noise. I have examined the locks and the windows—not even Houdini could have done it.

The ghost, having once established himself in Rita's bedroom, returned for additional visits—always in the early morning hours. Sometimes three times a week, sometimes even more often.

"He was staring in my direction all the time," Rita said with a slight Viennese accent, and one could see that the terror had never really left her eyes. Even three thousand miles away, the spectral stranger had a hold on the girl.

Was he perhaps looking for something? No, he didn't seem to be. In the kitchen, he either stood by the table or sat down on the counter. Ghosts don't need food—so why the kitchen?

"Did he ever take his hat off?" I wondered.

"No, never," she said and smiled. Imagine a ghost doffing his hat to the lady of the trailer!

What was particularly horrifying was the noiselessness of the apparition. She never heard any footfalls. No rustling of his clothes as he silently passed by. No clearing of the throat as if he wanted to speak. Nothing. Just silent stares. When the visitations grew more frequent, Rita decided to leave the lights on all night. After that, she did not *see* him any more. But he was still there, at the usual hour, standing behind the bed, staring at her. She knew he was. She could almost feel the sting of his gaze.

One night she decided she had been paying heavy light bills long enough. She hopped out of bed, turned the light switch to the off position, and as the room was plunged back into semidarkness, she lay down in bed again. Within a few moments, her eyes had gotten accustomed to the dark. Her senses were on the alert, for she was not at all sure what she might see. Finally, she forced herself to turn her head in the direction of the door. Was her mind playing tricks on her? There, in the doorway, stood the ghost. As big and brooding as ever.

With a scream, she dove under the covers. When she came up, eternities later, the shadow was gone from the door.

The next evening, the lights were burning again in the trailer, and every night thereafter, until it was time for her to fly to Germany for her season's nightclub work. Then she closed up the trailer, sent her children to stay with friends, and left, with the faint hope that on her return in the winter the trailer might be free of its ghost. But she wasn't at all sure.

It was getting dark outside now, and I knew Miss Atlanta had to fly back to Stuttgart for her evening's work soon. It was obvious to me that this exotic dancer was a medium, as only the psychic can "see" apparitions.

I queried her about the past, and reluctantly she talked of her earlier years in Austria.

When she was a school girl of eight, she suddenly felt herself impelled to draw a picture of a funeral. Her father was puzzled by the choice of so somber a subject by a little girl. But as she pointed out who the figures in her drawing were, ranging from her father to the more distant relatives, her father listened with lips tightly drawn. When the enumeration was over he inquired in a voice of incredulity mixed with fear, "But who is being buried?"

"Mother," the little girl replied, without a moment's hesitation, and no more was said about it.

Three weeks to the day later, her mother was dead.

The war years were hard on the family. Her father, a postal employee, had a gift for playing the numbers, allegedly upon advice from his deceased spouse. But the invasion by Germany ended all that and eventually Rita found herself in the United States and married to an Air Force Colonel.

She had forgotten her psychic experiences of the past, when the ghost in the trailer brought them all back only too vividly. She was frankly scared, knowing her abilities to receive messages from beyond the veil. But who was this man?

I decided to visit Peabody with a medium and see what we could learn, but it wasn't until the winter of the same year that I met Rita and she showed me around her trailer. It was a cold and moist afternoon.

Her oldest son greeted us at the door. He had seen nothing and neither believed nor disbelieved his mother. But he was willing to do some legwork for me, to find out who the shadowy visitor might be.

It was thus that we learned that a man had been run over by a car very close by, a few years ago. Had the dead man, confused about his status, sought refuge in the trailer—the nearest "house" in his path?

Was he trying to make contact with what he could sense was a medium, able to receive his anxious pleas?

It was at this time that I took the unusual photographs in Rita's presence of the areas indicated by her as being haunted. Several of these pictures show unusual mirrorlike areas, areas in which "something" must have been present in the atmosphere. But the ghost did not appear for me, or, for that matter, for Rita.

Perhaps our discovery of his "problem" and our long and passionate discussion of this had reached his spectral consciousness and he knew that he was out of his element in a trailer belonging to people not connected with his world.

Was this his way of finally, belatedly, doffing his hat to the lady of the house trailer with an apology for his intrusions?

I haven't had any further word from Rita Atlanta, but the newspapers carry oversize ads now and then telling this or that city of the sensational performance of the girl in the champagne glass.

It is safe to assume that she can take her bath in the glass completely alone, something she could not be sure of in the privacy of her Massachusetts trailer. For the eyes of a couple hundred visiting firemen in a Frankfurt nightclub are far less bothersome than one solitary pair of eyes staring at you from another world.

3

BANSHEES AND OMINOUS WARNINGS

I've been all over Ireland three times and have written a book called *The Lively Ghosts of Ireland*, but I've never met anyone in the Emerald Isle who had a banshee. Now there are things a Psychic Investigator considers legitimate and well-supported phenomena in the realm of the Uncanny, such as ghosts, haunted houses, and precognitive experiences.

Then, too, there are borderline cases involving phenomena of a more offbeat kind, such as the legendary stories about the Irish leprechauns and "little people," the fairies and brownies of Britain, and the dwarfs of Central Europe. To reject out of hand all such material as fantasy is of course no more scientific than to admit all spiritualist phenomena as genuine on the face of it without individual search and evaluation. What little we know of nature and our universe should have made us realize how much more there may be that is as yet unrevealed. A little humility can be most useful in modern science, but unfortunately the average physical scientist is filled with his own self-importance and has little patience with the bizarre.

The banshee is a Celtic spirit specializing in death warnings and they say it runs only in "old" Irish families. But I've heard of similar cases in other Celtic traditions and even outside of Britain. The banshee is usually described by those who actually have seen it as the figure of an ugly old woman, seated on the doorstep of the family about to be bereaved, and crying or screaming loudly. Banshees announce the forthcoming death of a member of the family without, however, telling the family who and when. That's part of the banshee game. Naturally the family is scared stiff when the banshee wails and everybody wonders who is next to go.

Died-in-the-wool Irish traditionalists will swear that banshees only run in the very good, ancient families and having one may be frightening, but it is also flattering: sort of a pedigree of death.

Now I have always been doubtful about the nature, though not the existence, of such strange creatures as elementals and banshees, considering them indeed part and parcel of ghostly manifestations, and thus human.

I've also learned that you can take the Irishman out of Ireland, but you can't take Ireland out of the Irishman. Even generations after, an Irish family transplanted into the New World may have the family banshee on their necks. Such is the case with the Shea family who live a pretty prosaic life in northern Massachusetts. Joanne Shea's grandmother, and even her mother, came from Ireland, as the song goes, and with them came accounts of strange goings-on whenever death was near for a member of the family.

The grandmother's particular banshee was mild in comparison to that of others: a strange creaking noise on the stairs, which she always tried to tell herself was natural, knowing full well, however, what it meant.

One day the grandmother was visiting Mrs. Shea and her sister and, upon leaving, startled the two girls by telling them it was her last visit. She would never see them again!

The family joked about this. Then two weeks later their grandmother fell and fractured her hip, and was hospitalized with the injury.

A few days afterwards, Mrs. Shea's sister, who is a nun, was standing by a window in her chapel. Suddenly she heard a terrible scream which she later described as sounding like the scream of a wildcat.

Terrified, she looked out the window, but could see nothing. Later, the two girls compared notes. At the exact moment when the nun had heard the scream, Grandmother had died.

A year went by. One evening, as Joanne lay in bed, she heard her brother's footsteps come up the stairs outside her room. Just then the clock chimed 11 P.M. To her surprise, Joanne clearly heard the footsteps of *two* people coming up the stairs, and wondered who the friend was her brother was bringing home at so late an hour. At the top of the stairs, the two pairs of footsteps separated, and one person went into the brother's room. The other footsteps came into Joanne's, and she suddenly felt petrified with fear.

Then all of a sudden, there, in front of her bed, stood her late grandmother.

Looking at the girl, the apparition turned her head a little, smiled—and then was gone like a puff of smoke.

When Joanne reported the matter to her mother the following morning, her mother brushed it aside as "probably a dream."

But then she stopped herself. What was the day's date? It was November 3—the anniversary of Grandmother's passing. Mother had forgotten to put Grandmother's name on the list of those for whom a prayer was to be said in church, as had been the custom in this Catholic family. The matter was immediately attended to, and when Joanne's brother came in that day, she questioned him about the other footsteps she had heard the night before.

He insisted that he had come in quite alone. He had not heard the ghostly steps either. Only Joanne had, and she never saw her late grandmother again after that.

Joanne's older sister, who was later to become a nun, evidently had also inherited the psychic talents so strong on the female side of the family tree.

One evening only the women were home, while the men— Joanne's father and her two brothers—were away at a ball game. Mother was downstairs, and the two girls were in bed in their room upstairs. Joanne was already beginning to doze off, when her sister suddenly jumped out of bed and ran downstairs to her mother's room.

"Did you hear the terrible scream?" the twenty-year-old girl asked her mother, who could only nod a silent yes. But Joanne had not heard it. It was a scream not unlike the cry of the wildcat, coming in from over the hill in back of the house. There was nothing outside in the yard to account for it.

For several days the women of the family were in a dither, waiting for fate to drop the other shoe. Everybody was told to be extremely careful and to avoid accidents. One could never know whom the banshee meant. On the eighth day after the unearthly scream had been heard, the waiting game was over. Joanne's uncle, her mother's brother, was hit by an automobile and died a few days later.

Just as the Germans have a peculiar name for the noisy ghost phenomena associated with disturbances of a physical nature which they call a *Poltergeist,* so they have a special term for the terrifying experience of a warning of impending death. These announcements of disaster or doom are called *Gaenger* in Central Europe, a word meaning, literally, "he who will go" (off stage), the stage being our physical world.

In a memorable but now very rare book called *"Gaenger, Geister und Gesichter"* ("Death Announcements, Ghosts and

Visions"), Friedrich von Gaggern reported some of these occurrences that were peculiarly tied in with the Germanic mood and landscape.

I was thinking of the Gaggern work when I first heard about Jane Marquardt of Rhode Island. Not so much because of her Germanic name—after all, it is her husband's—but because of the nature of the incidents that both enlivened and beclouded her life.

The most terrifying of these incidents took place when she was eighteen, at the time of World War II.

Her boy friend was a bombardier overseas, while she lived with her family in Chicago. One night she awoke from deep sleep with the sudden realization that someone was pounding on her bedroom door. There was no rational explanation for the loud knocks. She got up and checked the time. It was just 3 A.M. With a vague feeling of uneasiness, she returned to bed. Somehow she connected the uncanny knocks with her boy friend. He was due to return home soon, and they would be married.

Was it fear or the natural worry about a boy overseas in the war, or was it something more?

For two days Jane lived in a state of suspended animation. Then a telegram arrived with the tragic news that her boy friend had been killed. He and his buddies had safely completed their seventy-fourth mission and were returning home to their quarters in a bus. The bus went out of control and plunged over a cliff, killing the entire crew. Everyone on that bus was due for a furlough and return to the United States. The time of the accident was exactly 3 A.M., allowing for the difference in time zones.

The years went by and her shock wore off. She married another man, also in the military, and the family moved to New Jersey, where her husband was stationed. Jane was now twenty-five years old and the mother of a little girl. One evening they were coming back from a drive-in movie, and were within a few miles of their home, when she clearly saw a human face approaching the car on her side. As it drew near, she recognized her mother. Now she knew perfectly well that her mother was at that time in Chicago. Yet, there was her mother's face, smiling up at her and speaking to her in a clear and rather happy voice: "Jane, I'm going to die!"

With that, the vision faded quickly. Jane let out a scream. "No, dear God, no!"

Her husband, who had seen nothing, naturally assumed she was ill. Rather than alarm him, she kept her counsel. What was the point of telling him? she reasoned. Might it not *make* it happen in some unknown way? Also, she could tell by the way he cast sidelong glances at her, that he wondered about his wife's sanity.

Jane and her mother had always been very close and had kept in frequent contact over the miles. The vision occurred on a Tuesday at midnight. On Saturday Jane received an ominous telegram advising her of her mother's sudden death. The news hit her strongly and she took it badly. But later she realized that this had been her mother's way of softening the coming blow, by forewarning her of impending death. Had her own mother done this through subconscious channels? Had an agency *out there* created this vision for her benefit?

Jane was soon to learn more about her uncanny ability to tune in on distant dangers.

In 1952 she and her husband had to leave for Japan where he would hence be stationed. This was a heavy blow for her widowed father.

She was all he had left, for he, too, had taken his wife's passing badly. His tears of farewell seemed to stay in Jane's memory as she left for Japan.

She had not been in her new home more than three weeks when a strange thing happened. Her husband was downstairs, reading, while she was upstairs doing her nails. Their little girl was already asleep. Suddenly she heard clearly, so clearly it could have come from the next room, a voice calling her by name.

"Jane!" it said and at once she recognized her father's voice. She shook her head in bewilderment, wondering if she had imagined it due too her longing for her father. But again the voice called out to her. Now she dashed downstairs and questioned her husband about it. No, he had not called her. At this point she told him of her experience but he laughed it off.

A cable brought fearful news two days later. Her father had been taken ill and might not survive. But this time death did not exact the usual toll. After a long illness, Jane's father got well again. She checked the time of her experience with him and found that he had just had his first attack then. In desperation, he had actually called out to her, wishing she could be near him in this difficult hour. Somehow, his voice had traveled across the Pacific in a fraction of a second and reached his favorite daughter's ears—and only hers!

Mrs. V. works as a law secretary for a prominent attorney in the State of New Jersey. She never had any interest in the occult, but her innate psychic sense broke through eventually whether she wanted it or not. At first, there were just trifling things. Like handing her cleaner a pair of gloves and instantly knowing he would lose them. He did. Or looking for the gravestone of a friend in a cemetery she had never been to and finding it "blindly." Then, the night her mother died, she and her sister saw the lights in the living room go on by themselves. Since these were lights that had to be turned on individually, this was indeed unusual.

But on February 16, 1967, Mrs. V. had the shock of her life. It started as an ordinary working day. Her boss was dictating to her at her desk, which was located in a long hallway leading to his private offices. During a pause in the dictation, she looked up idly and saw, to her left, through a glass separation, a woman standing in the hall. The woman looked at her, and then moved quickly behind the elevator wall and out of her line of vision.

The woman was about twelve feet away and Mrs. V. saw her clearly through the glass. Her boss was part-owner of the building and often interviewed prospective tenants, so she assumed this was someone looking for office space and called his attention to the woman.

"Woman? What woman?" he demanded to know. "I don't see anyone."

"She has stepped behind the elevator wall," the secretary explained, somewhat sheepishly. The elevator is one of those older, noisy installations which one can hear approach quite clearly. Neither of them had heard the elevator coming up to the fourth floor, where they were, so they naturally felt the woman had still to be on the landing. But there was nobody there. Had she decided to walk down four flights—most unlikely in view of the elevator's presence—she could not have gotten far as yet. Also, in order to reach the stairwell, the woman would have had to brush past her employer.

Mrs. V. insisted there had been a visitor. The lawyer pressed the elevator button. The cab stopped at the fourth floor. It was empty. Evidently nobody had been riding it during the time of the incident, since the noise of the elevator's coming up could not have escaped them.

"You must have seen your own reflection in the glass partition," he reasoned. Some lawyers will reason peculiarly.

Mrs. V. shook her head. She knew what she had seen was not her own image. To prove her point, she re-enacted the whole thing. From the spot she had seen the woman stand, no reflection could be gleaned from inside the office.

The lawyer shrugged and went back to his work. Mrs. V. sat down quietly and tried to collect her thoughts. What had she seen? A woman of about sixty-five years of age, a little stocky in build, wearing a close-fitting hat and a brown, tweedy coat. Moreover, something about the woman's appearance seemed to be vaguely familiar. Then all at once it hit her who the woman was!

It was none other than her late mother, Mrs. T., who had been dead for thirteen years. She had owned a coat similar to the one Mrs. V. had seen and always favored close-fitting hats. Why had her mother's ghost appeared to her at this moment? she wondered.

Was it because her father was in ill health? Was this an omen, a warning of his impending death?

Grimly preparing for the unwanted, Mrs. V. went through her work rather mechanically for the next few days.

The following week, she received a phone call from one of her sisters. Her mother's favorite sister, their aunt, had suffered a stroke. One week to the day of her mother's appearance, Mrs. V.'s aunt was dead.

4

HOW IT FEELS TO BE A PROPHET

People have been saying things about the future ever since man realized he had a future. Some said it publicly and became prophets—or sometimes storm centers. Others, the majority in fact, who had "the gift," said it privately so that their loved ones might know. They were often considered oddballs. But the practitioners of the art of predicting went calmly on their way, for they could not help it. In Scotland they're called the fay people; in Holland the psychic researchers have dubbed them "paragnosts"; and in America we tend to refer to such people as being psychic. But in earlier periods they were often considered witches or somehow connected with the black arts—even though all they did was speak up when they had an impression of future events.

The ability to break through the time and space barrier is so common in man that I could cite thousands of verified examples to show that it does indeed exist and that it even has definite rules.

For instance, it works best when it is entirely spontaneous and not provoked deliberately. In fact, it rarely works in the laboratory and therefore all such tests are really a waste of time. Predictions and precognition are spontaneous phenomena, that is, they come to man rather than being the result of man's searching for them.

They are almost always connected with emotional situations, from death and danger to anticipation and joy, although they are more often sinister than pleasant. This stands to reason since danger is a deeper emotional experience than pleasure, and a lot more important to a man's life and well-being. I have written a book called *Predictions— Fact or Fallacy?* dealing with this subject in great detail.

The Psychic Investigator goes continually about his task of establishing proof that a nonphysical order of things exists around us and one cannot spend a single day without running into some form of prophecy or precognition experience somewhere, as the reports pour in.

While it is true that the average person cannot force the ability to predict future events to work when and as he wishes, there are professionals who have learned to discipline themselves to the point of opening their psychic doors at will, although not controlling what may come through them.

The celebrated Washington seeress Jeane Dixon has always held her "spontaneous" visions in much higher esteem than her "induced" crystal-ball gazing, although the latter "readings" have also produced some amazing, verified results dealing with future events. I am acquainted with Jeane Dixon, but it is with Betty Ritter and Ethel Johnson Meyers that I work most frequently in this area.

No medium or clairvoyante is good all the time and it can happen that a perfectly fine psychic can draw a blank once in a while, especially when the person requesting the reading makes her nervous or is unsympathetic. Relaxation is the key to all psychic perception, so it is easy to see how it matters what the person consulting the psychic is like.

Joy Todd is a young girl, a professional entertainer, who came to consult Mrs. Meyers at a time when her future was far from settled or certain. Mrs. Meyers knew nothing about the girl at the time, and in the winter of 1966 she applied her psychic talents to explore the girl's future for her. Miss Todd kept faithful records of all predictions made that day and has supplied me with the results.

"At the end of March or beginning of April you are going to sign a contract . . . it looks like you'll be out on the Coast."

Ethel was right. On March 29 Miss Todd left for Las Vegas and on April 1 signed a contract for the show called *That Certain Girl.*

"The activity will start in May and you'll be well into it by June. You'll be collecting money from it from then on in. It looks like a theatre and the bright lights will be on you. Some kind of musical, and you'll have a very good spot."

Rehearsals started on May 9, and they did open on June 21; Miss Todd did collect a salary every week from then on in. Performances were in a cabaret theatre with a proscenium arch and it was a musical comedy. Although the part was small it was a very good spot and the notices were excellent.

But Ethel's mental crystal ball was still full of information that day.

"I see you getting an offer from someone . . . it looks like RKO."

Not long afterward, a letter containing an offer to work in a new show arrived for Miss Todd. The name of the company? ARKO.

Turning now to more personal matters, Mrs. Meyers talked about what to a girl must be even more important than career matters: men.

"I see a man around you whom I like very much," she said, "and there seems to be a lot of building going on. He's going to become involved in some new activity. It's not in Philadelphia and not in New York either. Seems to be somewhere in between. And at the end of May this man will receive a large sum of money, something he has been waiting for."

To begin with, Mrs. Meyers had no way of knowing that the young girl before her was married and that her husband was in construction. Not long after the prediction was made by Mrs. Meyers, he did indeed start a new apartment building in Reading, Pennsylvania, which is certainly between New York and Philadelphia and not near either of these cities. Finally, on May 31 the husband received a large construction loan, for which he had indeed been waiting a long time.

"You will be busy during the summer," Mrs. Meyers added, "but he will be tied up, too . . . looks like more than one project."

Miss Todd was performing all summer long without interruption, while her husband was building two housing projects.

To Ethel Meyers clairvoyance is a calling and the fact that people pay her for her time—as well they should—not very important.

On the other end of the scale is the famous French seer Belline. To Monsieur Belline, the business of clairvoyance is strictly a business.

With him, everything is done very coldly: appointments are made through a staff secretary, and charges sent out as if it were all a medical consultancy. Monsieur himself wants to have nothing to do with the business part of it. He is independently wealthy from his books and magazine pieces and of course the fees for his time are substantial.

When we met him in the summer of 1967, we went to see him in a charming old house near the Montmartre section of the city.

We found Belline a neatly dressed, slight man, with a

French mustache, glasses, and looking more like a government clerk than a celebrated *voyant*.

He told us that he accidentally discovered his gift of being able to foretell the future at the age of fifteen. He does this in two ways: by merely getting into the atmosphere of the one he reads, and by palm reading. Combining a natural gift for psychology with flashes of genuine psychic intuition, Belline has become the psychic father confessor to troubled French men and women and his cases number in the thousands.

He is best known perhaps for his predictions about world events, which he makes from time to time and which are published by various important French newspapers and magazines.

One of the recent visions of Belline concerned the Near East. On October 7, 1966, Belline gave an interview to a small neighborhood newspaper called *La Liberté du Montmartre et du Centre,* in which he stated:

"I see soldiers, some blond, some dark, carrying the shield of David, with a six-pointed star, and who cross a frontier. I see the Jordan River and the numeral seventy-five."

Unlike Nostradamus, that other great French seer four centuries ago, Monsieur Belline also interprets his visions for his public.

"This is what I think it means," he said eight months before the Israeli-Arab war of 1967. "Preventive action by the armies of Israel at the risk of starting a Middle Eastern war. The Jordan seems to be the nerve center for their departure and Damascus, which is exactly seventy-five kilometers from the border, may be reached by Israeli commandos. The blond soldiers symbolize the Israelis of European origin, while the dark-skinned ones must be those of African and Yemenite origin."

The Israeli-Arab war took place on June 5, 1967, as is now common knowledge. Afterwards, Belline wondered whether the key figure 75 might not also have had other meanings. For example, 75 in the Bible is symbolic of "Divine alliance," for Abraham was 75 years old when God appeared to him and forged an alliance with the patriarch. Also, the date itself of the opening of hostilities—VI/5/1967—in numerology would be written down as 7 and 5, for it was the first day of the week, the sixth month of the year, and the fifth day of the month.

Be this as it may, nobody could foretell the course of history in the near East, when Belline had his vision.

At our meeting, Belline smiled and handed me copies of his two autobiographical books, one entitled *How I Became a Clairvoyant,* and the other, *Unusual Cases of a Clairvoyant.*

He repeated for my benefit a couple of dire predictions he had made a few days earlier in the French press.

"President Johnson will be in danger before the year is out," he said calmly, "I see him ill from the pressures of events, not going to his liking, and the possibility of an attenpt on his life. He will be incapacitated."

It was not the first prediction concerning the President's bad luck I had heard and of course people in the limelight are often the subject of such prophecies. Nevertheless, Belline was very sure of the details of this unfortunate turn of events and equally sure it would transpire by the end of 1968.

"I see an atomic explosion and atomic war in China before 1969," he continued, "somehow October 18, 1967, or 1968, might be important."

October 18, 1967, was very important to my wife. It was her birthday. Had our vibrations somehow gotten mixed up with the Chinese Reds?

Turning now to us, the affable prophet smiled and said, "The numerals 245 seem to have some meaning for you," and he added, "I see a road getting larger, with many branches . . . then a hole, but you already know about the hole, and the road goes on . . . then there is a house with lights and a large door . . . and a camera. You have trouble with your stomach and a weak leg."

"Anything else?" I interjected.

He smiled. "Keep your promises."

Well, the road that is getting larger is my increasing work load, and the hole, already known to me when we visited Belline in the late summer, was an extra tax bite I had to pay unexpectedly. But somehow I survived it and the road to success continued. The house with lights and camera is where we will make a motion picture soon, and I do have a nervous stomach and weak ankles. As for my promises, well, I have several deadlines to meet and I'm meeting them.

The figure 245, for which Monsieur offered no explanation other than he thought it had great meaning for me, adds up to an 11. Now every numerologist I know has always told me that 11 is my key number and whenever significant events take place in my life, there's an 11 in there some place in a prominent position. I find myself occupying airplane seats numbered 11 or getting calls at 11 A.M. that turn out important and my psychic camera takes just eleven exposures. I won't go on with my saga of figure 11. But judging from Monsieur Belline's own interpretation of the figure 75 in the Israeli war prediction, perhaps 245 also means a date in the future. Time alone will tell.

5

THE REALITY OF GHOSTS

It is all well and good to be hypnotizing people or to be recording their strange dreams and premonitions—then letting the skeptical world know what has come true and what has not—yet. But ghosts are a somewhat different matter. For one thing, as soon as you mention the word ghosts, everybody—well, almost everybody—gets set to hear a nice, chilling ghost *story*. Not an account of a psychic investigation with truth and deep significance. Ghosts that are *real*—why, that's upsetting! Especially if they happen to be the ghosts of relatives.

And yet, the facts are there for anyone with an uncommitted mind to study and ponder. Over the years I have had the opportunity of studying at first hand several thousand verified ghost cases. This does not of course include the many I put aside as being insufficiently supported by evidence or patently false. Just the real good ones.

But what exactly is a ghost? Something people dream up in their cups or on a sickbed? Something you read about in juvenile fiction? Far from it. Ghosts—apparitions of "dead" people or sounds associated with invisible human beings—are the surviving emotional memories of people. People who have not been able to make the transition from their physical body state into the world of spirit—or as Dr.

Joseph Rhine of Duke University has called it, the world of the *mind*. Their state is one of emotional shock induced by sudden death or great suffering and because of it the individuals involved cannot understand what is happening to them. They are unable to see beyond their own immediate environment or problem and are forced to relive continually those final moments of agony until someone breaks through and explains things to them. In this respect they are like psychotics being helped by the psychoanalyst, except that the patient is not on the couch, but in the atmosphere of destiny. Man's electromagnetic nature makes this perfectly plausible; that is, since our individual personality is really nothing more than a personal energy field encased in a denser outer layer called the physical body, the personality can store emotional stimuli and memories indefinitely without much dimming, very much like a tape recording that can be played over and over and does not lose clarity or volume.

Those who die normally under conditions of adjustment need not go through this agony, and they seem to pass on rapidly into that next state of consciousness that may be a "heaven" or a "hell," according to what the individual's mental state at death might have been. Neither state is an objective place, but is a subjective state of being. The sum total of similar states of being may, however, create a quasi-objective state approaching a condition or "place" along more orthodox religious lines. My contact with the confused individuals unable to depart beyond the earth's sphere, those who are commonly called "ghosts" or earthbound spirits, is through a trance medium who will lend her physical body temporarily to the entities in difficulty, so that they can speak through the medium and exteriorate their problems, frustrations, or unfinished business. Here again the parallel with psychoanalysis becomes apparent: in telling their tales of woe, the restless ones relieve themselves of their pressures and anxieties and thus may free themselves of their bonds. If fear is the absence of information, as I have always held, then knowledge is indeed the presence of understanding. Or the other way round, if you prefer. Because of my books, people often call on me to help them understand problems of this nature. Whenever someone has seen a ghost or heard noises of a human kind that do not seem to go with a body, and feel it might be something I ought to look into, I usually do.

To be sure, I don't always find a ghost. But I frequently do, and moreover, I find that many of those who have had the uncanny experiences are themselves mediumistic, and therefore capable of being communications carriers for the discarnates. It is more common than most people realize and really quite natural and harmless.

At times, it is sad and shocking, as all human suffering is, for man is his worst enemy, whether in the flesh or outside of it. But there is nothing mystical about the powers of ESP or the ability to experience ghostly phenomena.

Scoffers like to dismiss all ghostly encounters by cutting the witnesses down to size—their size. The witnesses are probably mentally unbalanced, they say, sick people who hallucinate a lot, or they were tired that day, or it must have been the reflection from (pick your light source), or finally, in desperation, they may say, yes, something probably happened to them, but in the telling they blew it all up so you can't be sure any more what really happened.

I love the way many people who cannot accept the possibility of ghosts being real toss out their views on what happened to strangers. "Probably this or that," and from "probably" it is only a short step, for them, to "certainly." The human mind is as clever at inventing away as it is at hallucinating. The advantage in being a scientifically trained reporter, as I am, is to be able to dismiss people's interpretations and find the facts themselves. I talked of the *Ghosts*

I've Met in a book a few years ago that bore that title. Even more fascinating are the people I've met who encounter ghosts. Are they sick, unbalanced, crackpots, or other unrealistic individuals whose testimony is worthless?

Far from it.

Those who fall into that category never get to me in the first place. They don't stand up under my methods of scrutiny. Crackpots, beware! I call a spade a spade, as I have proved when I exposed the fake spiritualist camp practices in print some years ago.

The people who come across ghostly manifestations are people like you.

Take the couple from Springfield, Illinois, for instance. Their names are Gertrude and Russell Meyers and they were married in 1935. He worked as a stereotyper on the local newspaper, and she was a high-school teacher. Both of them were in their late twenties and couldn't care less about such things as ghosts.

At the time of their marriage, they had rented a five-room cottage of no particular distinction but modest price, which had stood empty for some time. This was in Bloomington where the Meyerses then lived.

Gertrude Meyers came from a farm background and had studied at Illinois Wesleyan as well as the University of Chicago. For a while she worked as a newspaperwoman in Detroit, later taught school, and as a sideline has written a number of children's books. Her husband, Russell, also of farm background, attended Illinois State Normal University at Normal, Illinois, and later took his apprenticeship at the Bloomington Pantograph.

The house they had rented in Bloomington was exactly like the house next to it, and the current owners had converted what was formerly *one* large house into two separate units, laying a driveway between them.

After they had moved into their house, in the summer,

they went about the business of settling down to a married routine. Since her husband worked the night shift on the newspaper, Mrs. Meyers was often left alone in the house. At first, it did not bother her at all. Sounds from the street penetrated into the house and gave her a feeling of humanity nearby. But when the chills of autumn set in and the windows had to be closed to keep it out, she became aware, gradually, that she was not really alone on those lonely nights.

She had gone to bed one particular night early in their occupancy of the house, leaving her bedroom door ajar. It was ten-thirty and she was just about ready to go to sleep when she heard rapid, firm footsteps starting at the front door, inside the house, and coming through the living room, the dining room, and finally approaching her bedroom door down the hall leading to it.

She leapt out of bed and locked the bedroom door. Then she went back into bed and sat there, waiting in sheer terror what the intruder would do. But nobody came.

More to calm herself than because she really believed it, Mrs. Meyers convinced herself that she must have been mistaken about those footsteps.

Probably someone in the street. With this reassuring thought on her mind she managed to fall asleep.

The next morning, she did not tell her new husband about the nocturnal event. After all, she did not want him to think he had married a strange woman!

But the footsteps returned, night after night, many times, always at the same time and always stopping abruptly at her bedroom door, which, needless to say, she kept locked.

Rather than facing her husband with the allegation that they had rented a haunted house, she bravely decided to face the intruder and find out what this was all about. One night she deliberately waited for the now familiar, brisk footfalls. The clock struck ten, then ten-thirty. In the stillness of night, she could hear her heart pound in her chest.

The Reality of Ghosts • 51

Then the footsteps came. Closer, closer, until they got to her bedroom door. At this moment, Mrs. Meyers jumped out of bed, snapped on the light, and tore the door wide open.

There was nobody there, and no retreating footsteps could be heard.

She tried it again and again, but the invisible intruder never showed himself, once the door was opened.

The winter of 1936 was bitterly cold and it was Russell's habit of building up a fire in the furnace in the basement when he came home from work at 3:30 A.M. Mrs. Meyers always heard him come in, but did not get up. But one night he left the basement, came into the bedroom and said, "Why are you walking around this freezing house in the middle of the night?"

She of course had not been out of bed all night and told him as much. It was then that they discovered that he, too, had heard footsteps, but had thought it was his wife walking about the house restlessly. Meyers had heard the steps whenever he was fixing the furnace in the basement and by the time he got upstairs, they had ceased.

Mrs. Meyers had to get up early to go to her classes, but her husband would stay in the house sleeping late.

On many days he would hear someone walking about the house and investigate, only to find himself quite alone.

He would wake up in the middle of the night, thinking his wife had gotten up, but immediately reassured himself that she was sleeping peacefully next to him. Yet there was someone out there in the empty house! Since everything was locked securely, and countless attempts to trap the ghost had failed, the Meyerses shrugged and learned to live with their peculiar boarder.

Gradually the steps became part of the atmosphere of the old house, and the terror began to fade into the darkness of night.

In May of the following year, they decided to work the

garden, and as they did so, they met their next-door neighbors for the first time. Since they lived in identical houses, they had something in common, and conversation between them and the neighbors—a young man of twenty-five and his grandmother—sprang up.

Eventually the discussion got around to the footsteps. They, too, kept hearing them, it seemed. After they had compared notes on their experiences, the Meyerses asked some more questions. They were told that before the house was divided it belonged to a single owner. He had committed suicide in the house. No wonder he liked to walk in *both* halves of what was once his home!

You'd never think of Kokomo, Indiana, as particularly haunted ground, but one of the most touching cases I know of occurred there not long ago. A young woman by the name of Mary Elizabeth Hamilton was in the habit of spending many of her summer vacations in her grandmother's house there. The house dates back to 1834 and is a handsome place, meticulously kept up by the grandmother.

Miss Hamilton had never had the slightest interest in the supernatural and the events that transpired in the summer of 1964, when she spent four weeks at the house, came as a complete surprise to her. One evening she was walking down the front staircase when she was met by a lovely young lady coming up the stairs. Miss Hamilton, being a female, noticed that she wore a particularly beautiful evening gown. There was nothing about the woman the least bit ghostly, and she passed Miss Hamilton closely, so close in fact that she could have touched her, had she wanted to.

But she did notice that the gown was of a filmy, pink material, her hair dark brown and her eyes also brown. There were tears in those eyes. When the two women met, the girl in the evening gown smiled at Miss Hamilton and passed her.

Since she knew that there was no visitor in the house nor

anyone expected at this time, Miss Hamilton was puzzled as to who the lady might be. She turned her head to follow her up the stairs when she saw the lady in pink reach the top of the stairs—and vanish into thin air.

As soon as she could, she reported the matter to her grandmother, who shook her head and would not believe her account. She would not even discuss it, so Miss Hamilton let the matter drop out of deference for her grandmother. But the dress design had been so unusual, she decided to check it out in a library. She found to her amazement that the lady in pink had worn a dress of the 1847–1850 period.

In September of 1965 her grandmother decided to redecorate the house. In this endeavor she used many old pieces of furniture, some of which had come from the attic of the house. When Miss Hamilton arrived and saw the changes, she was suddenly stopped by a portrait hung in the hall.

It was a portrait of her lady of the stairs. She was not wearing the pink gown in this picture, but other than that, it was the same person.

Miss Hamilton's curiosity about the whole matter was again aroused and since she could not get any cooperation from her grandmother, she turned to her grandaunt for help. This was particularly fortunate since the aunt was a specialist in family genealogy.

Finally the lady of the stairs was identified. She turned out to be a much-removed cousin of Miss Hamilton's, who had once lived in this very house.

She had fallen in love with a ne'er-do-well, and after he died in a brawl, she threw herself down the stairs to her death.

Why had the family ghost picked on her to manifest, Miss Hamilton wondered.

Then she realized that there was a strong facial resemblance between her and the ghost. Moreover, their names were almost identical—Mary Elizabeth was Miss Hamilton's, and Elizabeth Mary the pink lady's. Both women had the same nickname, Libby.

Perhaps the ghost had looked for a little recognition from her family, and, having gotten none from the grandmother, had seized upon the opportunity of manifesting for a more amenable relative?

Miss Hamilton is happy that she was able to see the sad smile on the unfortunate girl's face, for to her it is proof that communication, though silent, took place between them across the years.

Mrs. Jane Eidson is a housewive in suburban Minneapolis. She is middle-aged and her children, five of them, range in age from nine to twenty. Her husband, Bill, travels four days each week. They live in a cottage-type brick house, which is twenty-eight years old, and they've lived there for the past eight years.

The first time the Eidsons noticed that there was something odd about their otherwise ordinary-looking home was after they had been in the house for a short time. Mrs. Eidson was in the basement, sewing, when all of a sudden she felt she was not alone and wanted to run upstairs. She suppressed this strong urge but felt very uncomfortable. One evening, later, her husband was down there practicing a speech when he had the same feeling of another presence. His self-control was not as strong as hers, and he came up the stairs. In discussing their strange feelings with their next-door neighbor they discovered that the previous tenant also had complained about the basement. Their daughter, Rita, never wanted to go to the basement by herself and, when pressed for a reason, finally admitted that there was a man down there. She described him as dark-haired and wearing a plaid shirt.

Sometimes he would stand at her bed at night and she would become frightened, but the moment she thought of calling her mother, the image disappeared. Another spot where she felt him was the little playhouse at the other end of their yard.

In the spring of 1966 Mrs. Eidson noticed a bouncing light at the top of the stairs as she was about to go to bed in an upstairs room, which she occupied due to her convalescing from surgery.

The light followed her to her room as if it had a mind of its own!

When she entered her room, the light left, but the room felt icy. She was disturbed by this, but nevertheless she went to bed and soon she had forgotten all about it as sleep came to her. Suddenly, in the middle of the night, she woke up and sat up in bed.

Something had awakened her. At the head of her bed she saw a man, "beige-colored" as she put it. As she stared at the apparition, it went away, leaving the room again very chilly.

About that time, too, the Eidsons noticed that their electric appliances were playing tricks on them. There was the time at 5 A.M. when their washing machine went on by itself. As did the television set in the basement, which could only be turned on by plugging it into the wall socket. When they had gone to bed, the set was off and there was no one around to plug it in.

Who was so fond of electrical gadgets as to turn them on in the small hours of the morning?

Finally Mrs. Edison found out. In May of 1949 a young man, just out of the service, had occupied their house. His hobby was electrical wiring, it seems, for he laid a strand of heavy wires from the basement underground through the yard to the other end of the property, where he attempted to hook them up with the utility pole belonging to the electric company. He was killed instantly. The spot was near where Mrs. Eidson's girl had seen the apparition. Since the wires are still in her garden, Mrs. Eidson is not at all surprised that the dead man likes to hang around.

And what better way for an electronics buff to manifest as a ghost than by appearing as a bright, bouncy light? As of this writing, the dead electrician is still playing tricks in the Edison home, and Mrs. Edison is looking for a new home— a little less unusual than their present one.

Eileen Courtis is forty-seven years old, a native of London, and a well-balanced individual who now resides on the West Coast but lived previously in New York City. Although she has never gone to College, she has a good grasp of things, an analytical mind, and is not given to hysterics. When she arrived in New York at age thirty-four, she decided to look for a quiet hotel and then for a job.

The job turned out to be an average office position, and the hotel she decided upon was the Martha Washington on Twenty-ninth Street, a hotel for women only. Eileen was essentially shy and a loner who made friends only slowly.

She was given a room on the twelfth floor.

Immediately on crossing the threshold she was struck by a foul odor coming from the room. Her first impulse was to ask for another room, but she was in no mood to create a fuss, so she stayed.

"I can stand it a night or two," she thought but did not unpack. It turned out that she stayed in that room for six long months, and yet she never really unpacked.

Now Eileen had had various experiences of what we now call extrasensory perception all her life, and her first impression of her new "home" was that someone had died in it. She examined the walls inch by inch. There was a spot where a crucifix must have hung for a long time, judging by the color of the surrounding wall. Evidently it had been removed when someone moved out . . . permanently.

That night, after she had gone to bed, her sleep was interrupted by what sounded like the turning of a newspaper page. It sounded exactly as if someone were sitting in the chair at the foot of her bed reading a newspaper. Quickly she switched on the light. She was of course quite alone. Were her nerves playing tricks on her? It was a strange city, a strange room. She decided to go back to sleep. Immediately the rustling started up again. And then someone was walking across the floor, starting from the chair toward the door of the room.

Eileen turned on every light in the room and it stopped. Exhausted, she dozed off again. The next morning she looked over the room carefully. Perhaps mice had caused the strange rustling. The strange odor remained, so she requested that the room be fumigated. The manager smiled wryly, and nobody came to fumigate her room and the rustling noise continued, night after night. Eileen slept with the lights on for the next three weeks.

Somehow her ESP told her this presence was a strong-willed, vicious old woman who resented others occupying what she still considered "her" room. Eileen decided to fight her. Night after night, she braved it out in the dark, only to find herself totally exhausted in the morning. Her appearance at the office gave rise to talk. But she was not going to give in to a ghost. Side by side, the living and the dead woman now occupied the same room without sharing it.

Then one night, something prevented her from going off to sleep. She lay in bed quietly, waiting.

Suddenly she became aware of two skinny but very strong arms extended over her head holding a large, well-filled downy pillow as though to suffocate her!

It took every ounce of her strength to force the pillow off her face.

Next morning, she tried to pass it off to herself as an hallucination. But was it? She was quite sure that she had not been asleep.

But still she did not move out and one evening when she arrived home from the office with a friend, she felt a sudden pain in her back, as if she had been stabbed. During the night, she awoke to find herself in a state of utter paralysis. She could not move her limbs or head. Finally, after a long time, she managed to work her way to the telephone receiver and call for a doctor. Nobody came. But her control seemed to start coming back, and she called her friend, who rushed over only to find Eileen in a state of shock.

During the next few days she had herself thoroughly examined by the company physician, including the taking of X-rays, to determine if there was anything physically wrong with her that could have caused this condition. She was given a clean bill of health. Her strength had by then returned and she decided to quit while she was ahead.

She went to Florida for an extended rest, but eventually came back to New York and the hotel again. This time she was given another room, where she lived very happily and without incident for over a year.

One day a neighbor who knew her from the time she had occupied the room on the twelfth floor saw her in the lobby and insisted on having a visit with her. Reluctantly, for she is not fond of socializing, Eileen agreed. The conversation covered various topics until suddenly the neighbor came out with "the time you were living in that haunted room across the hall."

Since Eileen had never told anyone of her fearsome experiences there, she was puzzled. The neighbor confessed that she had meant to warn her while she was occupying that room, but somehow never had mustered enough courage. "Warn me of what?" Eileen insisted.

"The woman who had the room just before you moved in," the neighbor explained haltingly, "well, she was found dead in the chair, and the woman who had it before her also was found dead, in the bathtub."

Eileen swallowed quickly, and left. Suddenly she knew that the pillowcase had not been a hallucination.

One of the most bizarre ghost stories concerns an event

which actually happened in my wife's family. It is so strange that I would take it with more than a grain of salt if I did not know the people involved so well. As it is, the chief witness is very much alive—my brother-in-law, Count Anatol Buxhoeveden, who was only a youngster when it happened, but who was left with a very lasting impression, the details of which are very clear in his mind.

The Buxhoeveden family is one of the oldest noble families of Europe, related to a number of royal houses and—since the eighteenth century when one of the Counts married the daughter of Catherine the Great of Russia—also to the Russian Imperial family. The family seat was Lode Castle on the island of Oesel, off the coast of Estonia. The castle, which is still standing, is a very ancient building, with a round tower somewhat apart from the main building. Its Soviet occupiers have since turned it into a museum.

The Buxhoevedens acquired it when Frederick William Buxhoeveden married Natalie of Russia, as a gift from mother-in-law Catherine.

Thus it was handed down from first-born son to first-born son, until it came to be in the hands of an earlier Count Anatol Buxhoeveden. The time was the beginning of this century, and all was well with the world.

Estonia was a Russian province, so it was not out of the ordinary that Russian regiments should hold war games in the area, and on one occasion the maneuvers were in full swing, when the regimental commander requested that his officers be put up at the castle. The soldiers were located in the nearby town, but five of the staff officers came to stay at Lode Castle. Grandfather Buxhoeveden was the perfect host, dining and wining them, but unhappy that he could not accommodate all five in the main house. The fifth man would have to be satisfied with quarters in the tower. Since the tower had by then acquired a reputation of being haunted, he asked for a volunteer to stay in that particular room.

There was a great deal of teasing about the haunted room before the youngest of the officers volunteered and left for his quarters.

The room seemed cozy enough and the young officer congratulated himself for having chosen so quiet and pleasant a place to spend the night after a hard day's maneuvers.

And, tired as he was, he decided to get into bed right away. But he was too tired to fall asleep quickly, so he took a book from one of the shelves lining the walls, lit the candle on his night table, and began to read for a while.

As he did so, he suddenly became aware of a greenish light toward the opposite end of the circular room. As he looked at the light with astonishment, it changed before his eyes into the shape of a woman. She seemed solid enough and to his horror came over to his bed, taking him by the hand and demanding that he follow her. Somehow he could not resist her commands, even though not a single word was spoken. He followed her down the stairs into the library in the castle itself. There she made signs indicating that he was to remove the carpet. Without questioning her, he flipped back the rug. She then pointed at a trap door that had appeared underneath the carpet. He opened the door and followed the figure down a flight of stairs until they came to a big iron door that barred their progress. Now the figure pointed to the right corner of the floor and he dug into it. There he found a key, perhaps ten inches long, and with it he opened the iron gate. He now found himself in a long corridor which he followed and which led him to a circular room. From there another corridor led on and again he followed eagerly, wondering what this was all about.

This latter corridor suddenly gave onto another circular room which seemed familiar—he was back in his own room. The apparition was gone.

What did it all mean? He sat up trying to figure it out and when he finally dozed off it was already dawn. Consequently he overslept and came down to breakfast last. His state of excitement immediately drew the attention of the Count and his fellow officers. "You won't believe this," he began and told them what had happened to him.

He was right. Nobody believed him.

But his insistence that he was telling the truth was so convincing that the Count finally agreed, more to humor him than because he believed him, to follow the young officer to the library to look for the alleged trap door.

"But," he added, "I must tell you that on top of that carpet are some heavy bookshelves filled with books which have not been moved or touched in over a hundred years. It is quite impossible for any one man to flip back that carpet."

They went to the library and just as the Count had said, the carpet could not be moved. But Grandfather Buxhoeveden decided to follow through anyway and called in some of his men. Together, ten men were able to move the shelves and turn the carpet back. Underneath the carpet was a dust layer one inch thick, but it did not stop the intrepid young officer from looking for the ring of the trap door. After a long search for it, he finally located it. A hush fell over the group when he pulled the trap door open. There was the secret passage and the iron gate. And there, next to it, was a rusty iron key. The key fit the lock. The gate, which had not moved for centuries perhaps, slowly and painfully swung open and the little group continued their search of the musty passages. With the officer as leader, the men went through the corridors and came out in the tower room, just as he had done during the night.

But what did it mean? Everyone knew there were secret passages—lots of old castles had them as a hedge in time of war.

The matter gradually faded from memory and life at Lode

went on. The iron key, however, was preserved and remained in the Buxhoeveden family until some years ago, when it was stolen from Count Alexander's Paris apartment.

Ten years went by until, after a small fire in the castle, Count Buxhoeveden decided to combine the necessary repairs with the useful installation of central heating, something old castles always need. The contractor doing the job brought in twenty men who worked hard to restore and improve the appointments at Lode. Then one day, the entire crew vanished to a man—like ghosts. Count Buxhoeveden reported this to the Police, who were already being besieged by the wives and families of the men who had disappeared without leaving a trace.

Newspapers of the period had a field day with the case of the vanishing workmen, but the publicity did not help to bring them back, and the puzzle remained.

Then, came the revolution and the Buxhoevedens lost their ancestral home. Count Alexander and the present Count Anatol, my brother-in-law, went to live in Switzerland. The year was 1923. One day the two men were walking down a street in Lausanne, when a stranger approached them, calling Count Alexander by name.

"I am the brother of the Major Domo of your castle," the man explained, "I was a plumber on that job of restoring it after the fire."

So much time had passed and so many political events had changed the map of Europe that the man was ready at last to lift the veil of secrecy from the case of the vanishing workmen.

This is the story he told: When the men were digging trenches for the central heating system, they accidentally came across an iron kettle of the kind used in the Middle Ages to pour boiling oil or water down on the enemies besieging a castle. But this pot was not full of water but of gold. They had stumbled onto the long-missing Buxhoevden treasure, a hoard reputed to have existed for centuries but never found. Now, at this stroke of good fortune, the workmen became larcenous. To a man, they opted for distributing the find among themselves, even though it meant leaving everything behind—their families, their homes, their work—and striking out fresh somewhere else. But the treasure was large enough to make this a pleasure rather than a problem, and they never missed their wives, it would seem, finding ample replacements in the gentler climes of western Europe, where most of them went to live under assumed names.

At last the apparition that had appeared to the young officer made sense: an ancestor who wanted to let her descendants know where the family gold had been secreted. What a frustration for a ghost to see her efforts come to naught, and worse yet, to see the fortune squandered by thieves while the legal heirs had to go into exile. Who knows how things might have turned out for the Buxhoevedens if *they* had gotten to the treasure in time.

At any rate there is a silver lining to this account: since there is nothing further to find at Lode Castle, the ghost does not have to put in appearances under that ghastly new regime. But Russian aristocrats and English lords of the manor have no corner on uncanny phenomena. Nor are all of the haunted settings I have encountered romantic or forbidding. Certainly there are more genuine ghostly manifestations in the American Midwest and South than anywhere else in the world. This may be due to the fact that a great deal of violence occurred there during the nineteenth and early twentieth centuries. Also, the American public's attitude toward the phenomena is different from that of Europeans. In Europe, people are inclined to reserve their accounts of bona fide ghosts for those they can trust. Being ridiculed is not a favorite pastime with most Europeans.

Americans, by contrast, are more independent. They couldn't care less what others think of them in the long run, so long as their own people believe them. I have approached individuals in my cases with an assurance of scientific inquiry and respect for their stories. I am not a skeptic. I am a searcher for truth, regardless of what this truth looks or sounds like.

A short time ago a well-known TV personality took issue with me concerning my conviction that ESP and ghosts are real. Since he was not well informed on the subject he should not have ventured forth into an area I know so well. He proudly proclaimed himself a skeptic.

Irritated, finally, I asked him if he knew what being a skeptic meant. He shook his head.

"The term skeptic," I lectured him patiently, "is derived from the Greek word *skepsis,* which was the name of a small town in Asia Minor in antiquity. It was known for its lack of knowledge and people from skepsis were called skeptics."

The TV personality didn't like it at all, but the next time we met on camera, he was a lot more human and his humility finally showed.

In May of 1965 I received a curious letter from a Mrs. Stewart living in Chicago, Illinois, in which she explained that she was living with a ghost and didn't mind, except that she had lost two children at birth and this ghost was following not only her but also her little girl. This she didn't like, so could I please come and look into the situation?

I could and did. On July 4 I celebrated Independence Day by trying to free a hung-up lady ghost on Chicago's South Side. The house itself was an old one, built around the late 1800s, and not exactly a monument of architectural beauty. But its functional sturdiness suited its present purpose—to house a number of young couples and their children, people who found the house both convenient and economical.

In its heyday, it had been a wealthy home, complete with servants and backstairs for them to go up and down on. The three stories are even now connected by an elaborate buzzer system, which, however, hasn't worked for years.

I did not wish to discuss the phenomena at the house with Mrs. Stewart until after Sybil Leek, who was with me, had had a chance to explore the situation. My good friend Carl Subak, a stamp dealer, had come along to see how I worked. He and I had known each other thirty years ago when we were both students and because of that he had overcome his own—ah—skepticism—and come along. Immediately on arrival Sybil ascended the stairs to the second floor as if she knew where to go! Of course she didn't; I had not discussed the matter with her at all. But despite this promising beginning, she drew a complete blank when we arrived in the apartment upstairs. "I feel absolutely nothing," she confided and looked at me doubtfully. Had I made a mistake? she seemed to ask. On a hot July day, come all the way to the South Side of Chicago on a wild ghost chase?

We gathered in a bedroom where there was a comfortable chair, and windows on both sides of the room that gave onto an old-fashioned garden; there was a porch on one side and a parkway on the other. The furniture, in keeping with the modest economic circumstances of the owners, was old and worn, but it was functional and they did not seem to mind.

In a moment, Sybil Leek had slipped into trance. But instead of a ghost's personality, the next voice we heard was Sybil's own, although it sounded strange. Sybil was "out" of her own body, but able to observe the place and report back to us while still in trance.

The first thing she saw were maps, in a large round building somehow connected with the house we were in.

"Is there anyone around?" I asked.

"Yes," Sybil intoned, "James Dugan."

"What does he do here?"

"Come back to live."

"When was that?"

"1912."

"Is there anyone with him?"

"There is another man. McCloud."

"Anyone else?"

"Lots of people."

"Do they live in this house?"

"Three, four people . . . McCloud . . . maps . . ."

"All men?"

"No . . . girl . . . Judith . . . maidservant . . ."

"Is there an unhappy presence here?"

"Judith . . . she had no one here, no family . . . that man went away . . . Dugan went away . . ."

"How is she connected with this Dugan?"

"Loved him."

"Were they married?"

"No. Lovers."

"Did they have any children?"

There was a momentary silence, then Sybil continued in a drab, monotonous voice.

"The baby's dead."

"Does she know the baby's dead?"

"*She cries . . . baby cries . . .* neglected . . . by Judith . . . guilty . . ."

"Does Judith know this?"

"Yes."

"How old was the baby when it died?"

"A few weeks old."

Strange, I thought, that Mrs. Stewart had fears for her own child from this source. She, too, had lost children at a tender age.

"What happened to the baby?"

"She put it down the steps."

"What happened to the body then?"

"I don't know."

"Is Judith still here?"

"She's here."

"Where?"

"This room . . . and up and down the steps. She's sorry for her baby."

"Can you talk to her?"

"No. She cannot leave here until she finds— You see if she could get Dugan—"

"Where is Dugan?"

"With the maps."

"What is Dugan's work?"

"Has to do with roads."

"Is he dead?"

"Yes. She wants him here, but he is not here."

"How did she die?"

"She ran away to the water . . . died by the water . . . but is here where she lived . . . baby died on the steps . . . downstairs . . ."

"What is she doing here, I mean how does she let people know she is around?"

"She pulls things . . . *she cries* . . ."

"And her Christian name?"

"Judith Vincent, I think. Twenty-one. Darkish, not white. From an island."

"And the man? Is he white?"

"Yes."

"Can you see her?"

"Yes."

"Speak to her?"

"She doesn't want to, but perhaps . . ."

"What year does she think this is?"

"1913."

"Tell her this is the year 1965."

Sybil informed the spirit in a low voice that this was 1965 and she need not stay here any longer. Dugan is dead, too.

"She has to find him," Sybil explained and I directed her

to explain that she need only call out for her lover in order to be reunited with him Over There.

"She's gone . . ." Sybil finally said, and breathed deeply.

A moment later she woke up and looked with astonishment at the strange room, having completely forgotten how we got here, or where we were.

There was no time for explanations now, as I still wanted to check out some of this material. The first one to sit down with me was the owner of the flat, Mrs. Alexandra Stewart. A graduate of the University of Iowa, twenty-five years old, Alexandra Stewart works as a personnel director. She had witnessed the trance session and seemed visibly shaken. There was a good reason for this. Mrs. Stewart, you see, had met the ghost Sybil had described.

The Stewarts had moved into the second floor apartment in the winter of 1964. The room we were now sitting in had been hers. Shortly after they moved in, Mrs. Stewart happened to be glancing up toward the French doors, when she saw a woman looking at her. The figure was about five feet three or four, and wore a blue-gray dress with a shawl, and a hood over her head, for which reason, Mrs. Stewart could not make out the woman's features. The head seemed strangely bowed to her, almost as if the woman were doing penance.

I questioned Mrs. Stewart on the woman's color in view of Sybil's description of Judith. But Mrs. Stewart could not be sure; the woman could have been white or colored. At the time Mrs. Stewart had assumed it to be a reflection from the mirror, but when she glanced at the mirror, she did not see the figure in it. When she turned her attention back to the figure, it had disappeared. It was toward evening, and Mrs. Stewart was a little tired, yet the figure was very real to her. And her doubts were completely dispelled when the ghost returned about a month later. In the meantime she had had the dresser that had stood in the line of sight moved farther down, so that any reflection as explanation would simply not hold water. Again the figure appeared at the French doors. She looked very unhappy to Mrs. Stewart, who felt herself strangely drawn to the woman, almost as if she should help her in some as yet unknown way.

But the visual visitations were not all that disturbed the Stewarts. Soon they were hearing strange noises, too. There was, above all, the crying of a baby, which seemed to come from the second-floor rear bedroom. It could also be heard, though less loud, in the kitchen and seemed to come from the walls. Several people had heard it and there was no natural cause to account for it. And then there were the footsteps. Someone walking down the backstairs, the servants' stairs, step by step, hesitatingly, and not returning, but just fading away!

They dubbed their ghostly guest "Elizabeth," for want of a better name. Mrs. Stewart did not consider herself psychic nor did she have any interest in such matters. But occasionally things had happened to her that defied natural explanations. Such as the time just after she had lost a baby. She awoke from a heavy sleep with the intangible feeling of a presence in her room. She looked up and there, in the rocking chair across the room, she saw the woman, now dead, who had taken care of her when she was a child herself. Rocking gently in the chair, as if to reassure her, the Nanny held Mrs. Stewart's baby in her arms. In a moment, the vision was gone, but it had left Alexandra Stewart with a sense of peace. She knew her little one was well looked after.

The phenomena continued, however, and soon were no longer restricted to the upstairs. On the first floor, in the living room, Mrs. Stewart heard the noise of someone breathing close to her. This had happened only recently, again in the presence of her husband and a friend. She asked them to hold their breath for a moment, and still she heard the strange breathing continue as before. Neither of the men could hear it. Or so they said. But the following day the guest came back with another man. He wanted to be sure of his observation before admitting that he too had heard the invisible person breathe close to him.

The corner of the living room where the breathing had been heard was also the focal point for strange knockings that faulty pipes could not explain. On one occasion, they heard the breaking of glass, and yet there was no evidence that any glass had been broken. There was a feeling that someone other than the visible people was present at times in their living room and it made them a little nervous even though they did not fear their "Elizabeth."

Alexandra's young husband grew up in the building trade, and now works as a photographer. He too has heard the footsteps on many occasions, and he knew the difference between them and a house settling or timbers creaking— these were definitely human noises.

Mrs. Martha Vaughn is a bookkeeper who had lived in the building for two years at that time. Hers is the apartment in the rear portion of the second floor, and it includes the back porch. Around Christmas of 1964 she heard a baby crying on the porch. It was a particularly cold night, so she went to investigate immediately. It was a weird, unearthly sound— to her it seemed right close by the porch, but there was no-body around. The yard was deserted. The sound to her was the crying of a small child, not of a baby, but perhaps a child of from one to three years of age. The various families shared the downstairs living room "like a kibbutz," as Mrs. Stewart put it, so it was not out of the ordinary for several people to be in the downstairs area. On one such occasion Mrs. Vaughn also heard the breaking of the *invisible* glass.

Richard Vaughn is a laboratory technician. He too has heard the baby cry and the breaking of the glass that isn't there; he has heard pounding on the wall as have the others. A skeptic at first, he tried to blame these noises on the steam-pipes that heat the house. But when he listened to the pipes when they were acting up, he realized at once that the noises he had heard before were completely different.

"What about a man named Dugan? Or someone having to do with maps?" I asked.

"Well," Vaughn said, and thought back, "I used to get mail here for people who once lived here, and of course I sent it all back to the post office. But I don't recall the name Dugan. What I do recall was some mail from a Washington Bureau. You see, this house belongs to the University of Chicago and a lot of professors used to live here."

"Professors?" I said with renewed interest.

Was Dugan one of them?

Several other people who lived in the house experienced strange phenomena. Barbara Madonna used to live there too. But in May of 1964 she moved out. She works three days a week as a secretary and moved into the house in November of 1963. She and her husband much admired the back porch when they first moved in and had visions of sitting out there drinking a beer on warm evenings. But soon their hopes were dashed by the uncanny feeling they were not alone, of another presence in their apartment, especially around the porch. Soon, instead of using the porch, they studiously avoided it, even if it meant walking downstairs to dust out a mop. Theirs was the third-floor apartment, directly above the Stewart apartment.

A girl by the name of Lolita Krol also had heard the baby crying. She lived in the building for a time and bitterly complained about the strange noises on the porch.

Douglas McConnor is a magazine editor, and he and his wife moved into the building in November of 1964, first to the second floor and later to the third. From the very first, when McConnor was still alone—his wife joined him in the flat after their marriage a little later—he felt extremely uncomfortable in the place. Doors and windows would fly open by themselves when there wasn't any strong wind.

When he moved upstairs to the next floor, things were much quieter, except for one thing: always on Sunday nights, noisy activities would greatly increase toward midnight. Footsteps, the sounds of people rushing about and of doors opening and closing would disturb Mr. McConnor's rest. The stairs were particularly noisy. But when he checked he found that everybody was accounted for, and that no living person had caused the commotion.

It got to be so bad he started to hate Sunday nights.

I recounted Sybil's trance to Mr. McConnor and the fact that a woman named Judith had been the central figure of it.

"Strange," he observed, "but the story also fits my ex-wife who deserted her children. She is of course very much alive now. Her name is Judith."

Had Sybil intermingled the impression of a dead maid-servant with the imprint left behind by an unfit mother? Or were there two Judiths? At any rate the Stewarts did not complain further about uncanny noises and the girl in the blue-gray dress never came back.

On the way to the airport Carl Subak seemed unusually silent as he drove us out to the field.

What he had witnessed seemed to have left an impression on him and his philosophy of life.

"What I find so particularly upsetting," he finally said, "is Sybil's talking about a woman and a dead baby—all of it borne out afterwards by the people in the house. But Sybil did not know this. She couldn't have."

No, she couldn't.

In September of 1967, a group consisting of a local television reporter, a would-be psychic student and an assortment of clairvoyants descended on the building in search of psychic excitement. All they got out of it were more mechanical difficulties with their cameras. But the ghosts had, of course, left long before.

Ghosts are not just the privilege of the thrill seekers or the hallucinations of disturbed people. Nothing is as democratic as seeing or hearing a ghost, for it happens all the time to just about every conceivable type of person. Neither age nor race nor religion seem to stay these spectral people in their predetermined haunts.

Naturally I treat each case reported to me on an individual basis. Some I reject on the face of the report and others only after I have been through a long and careful investigation. But other reports have the ring of truth about them and are worthy of belief, even though some of them are no longer capable of verification because witnesses have died or sites destroyed.

A good example is the case reported to me recently by a Mrs. Edward Needs, Jr., of Canton, Ohio. In a small town by the name of Homeworth, there is a stretch of land near the highway that is today nothing more than a neglected farm with a boarded-up old barn still standing. The spot is actually on a dirt road, and the nearest house is half a mile away, with wooded territory in between. This is important, you see, for the spot is isolated and a man might die before help could arrive. . . . On rainy days, the dirt road is impassable. Mrs. Needs has passed the spot a number of times, and does not particularly care to go there. Somehow it always gives her an uneasy feeling. Once, the Needs's car got stuck in the mud on a rainy day, and they had to drive through open fields to get out.

It was on that adventure-filled ride that Mr. Needs confided for the first time what had happened to him at that spot on prior occasions. The year was 1961 when Edward Needs and a friend were on a joy ride after dark. At that time Needs had not yet married his present wife, and the two men had been drinking a little, but were far from drunk.

It was then that they discovered the dirt road for the first time.

On the spur of the moment, they followed it. A moment later they came to the old barn. But just as they were approaching it, a man jumped out of nowhere in front of them. What was even more sobering was the condition this man was in: engulfed in flames from head to toe!

Quickly Needs put his bright headlights on the scene, the better to see. The man now ran into the woods across the road, and just disappeared.

Two men never became cold sober more quickly. They turned around and went back to the main highway fast. But the first chance they had, they returned with two carloads full of other fellows. They were equipped with strong lights, guns, and absolutely no whiskey. When the first of the cars was within twenty feet of the spot where Needs had seen the apparition, they all saw the same thing: There before them, was the horrible spectacle of a human being blazing from top to bottom and evidently suffering terribly as he tried to run away from his doom. Needs emptied his gun at the figure: it never moved or acknowledged that it had been hit by the bullets. A few seconds later, the figure ran into the woods—exactly as it had when Needs had first encountered it.

Now the ghost posse went into the barn, which they found abandoned, although not in very bad condition. The only strange thing was spots showing evidence of fire: evidently someone or something had burned inside the barn without, however, setting fire to the barn as a whole. Or had the fiery man run outside to save his barn from the fire?

Betty Ann Tylaska lives in a seaport in Connecticut. Her family is a prominent family going back to Colonial days, and they still occupy a house built by her great-great-great-grandfather, for his daughter and her husband, back in 1807.

In 1961 Mrs. Tylaska and her husband, a Navy officer,

were in the process of restoring the venerable old house to its former glory. Neither of them had the slightest interest in the supernatural, and to them such things as ghosts simply did not exist except in children's tales.

The first time Mrs. Tylaska noticed anything unusual was one night when she was washing dishes in the kitchen.

Suddenly she had the strong feeling that she was being watched. She turned around and caught a glimpse of a man standing in the doorway between the kitchen and the living room of the downstairs part of the house. She saw him only for a moment, but long enough to notice his dark blue suit and silver buttons. Her first impression was that it must be her husband, who, of course, wore a Navy blue uniform. But on checking she found him upstairs, wearing entirely different clothes.

She shrugged the matter off as probably a hallucination due to her tiredness. But the man in blue kept returning. On several occasions, the same uncanny feeling of being watched came over her, and when she turned around, there was the man in the dark blue suit.

It came as a relief to her when her mother confessed that she too had seen the ghostly visitor—always at the same spot, between living room and kitchen. Finally she informed her husband and to her surprise he did not laugh at her. But he suggested that if it was a ghost, perhaps one of her ancestors was checking up on them.

Perhaps he wanted to make sure they restored the house properly and did not make any unwanted changes. They were doing a great deal of painting in the process of restoring the house, and whatever paint residue was left, they would spill against an old stone wall in the back of the house.

Gradually the old stones were covered with paint of various hues.

One day, Mr. Tylaska found himself in front of these stones. For want of anything better to do at the moment, he started to study them. To his amazement, he discovered that one of the stones was different from the others: it was long and flat. He called his wife and they investigated the strange stone; upon freeing it from the wall, they saw to their horror that it was a gravestone—her great-great-great-grandfather's tombstone, to be exact.

Inquiry at the local church cleared up the mystery of how the tombstone had gotten out of the cemetery. It seems that all the family members had been buried in a small cemetery nearby. But it filled up, and one day a larger cemetery was started. The bodies were removed to it and a larger monument erected over great-great-great-grandfather's tomb. Since the original stone was of no use any longer, it was left behind. Somehow the stone got used when the old wall was being built. Evidently great-great-great-grandfather did not like the idea. Was that the reason for his visits? After all, who likes having paint splashed on one's precious tombstone? I ask you.

The Tylaska family held a meeting to decide what to do about it. They could not very well put two tombstones on grandad's grave. What would the other ancestors think? Everybody would want to have two tombstones then; and while it might be good news to the mason, it would not be a thing to do in practical New England.

So they stood the old tombstone upright in their own backyard. It was nice having grandad with them that way and if he felt like a visit, why, that was all right with them too.

From the moment when they gave the tombstone a place of honor, the gentleman in the dark blue suit and the silver buttons never came back. But Mrs. Tylaska does not particularly mind. Two Navy men in the house might have been too much of a distraction anyway.

Give a ghost his due, and he'll be happy. Happy ghosts don't stay around: in fact, they turn into normal spirits, free to come and go, mostly go, at will. But until people come to recognize that the denizens of the Other World are real people like you and I and not some benighted devils or condemned souls in a purgatory created for the benefit of a political church, people will be frightened of ghosts quite needlessly. Sometimes even highly intelligent people shudder when they have a brush with the uncanny. Take young Mr. Bentine, for instance, the son of my dear friend Michael Bentine, the British TV star, and, like his father, very much interested in the psychic. But young Bentine never bargained for firsthand experiences.

It happened at school, Harrow, one of the finest British "public schools" (in America they are called private schools), in the spring of 1966. Young Bentine lived in a dormitory known as The Knoll. One night around 2 A.M. he awoke from sound sleep. The silence of the night was broken by the sound of footsteps coming from the headmaster's room. The footsteps went from the room to a nearby bathroom and then suddenly came to a halt. Bentine thought nothing of it, but why had it awakened him? Perhaps he had been studying too hard and it was merely a case of nerves. At any rate he decided not to pay any attention to the strange footsteps. After all, if the headmaster wished to walk at that ungodly hour, that was his business and privilege.

But the following night, the same thing happened. Again, at 2 A.M., he found himself awake, and there came the ominous footsteps. Again they stopped abruptly when they reached the bathroom. Coincidence? Cautiously young Bentine made some inquiries. Was the headmaster given to nocturnal walks perhaps? He was not.

The third night, Bentine decided that if it happened again, he would be brave and look into it. He fortified himself with some tea and then went to bed. It was not easy falling asleep but eventually his tiredness won the upper hand and our young man was asleep in his room.

Promptly at two, however, he was awake again. And quicker than you could say, "Ghost across the hall," there were the familiar footsteps!

Quickly our intrepid friend got up and stuck his head out of his door, facing the headmaster's room and the bathroom directly across the corridor.

The steps were now very loud and clear. Although he did not see anyone, he heard someone or something move along the passage.

He was petrified. As soon as the footsteps had come to the usual abrupt halt in front of the bathroom door, he crept back into his own room and bed. But sleep was out for the night. The hours were like months, until finally morning came and a very tired Bentine went down to breakfast, glad the ordeal of the night had come to an end.

He had to know what this was all about, no matter what the consequences. To go through another night like that was out of the question.

He made some cautious inquiries about that room. There had been a headmaster fourteen years ago in that room who had died there. Suicide it was, and he had hanged himself in the shower of the bathroom. Bentine turned white as a ghost himself when he heard the story. He immediately tried to arrange to have his room changed. But that could not be done as quickly as he had hoped, so it was only after another two and a half weeks that he was able to banish the steps of the ghostly headmaster from his mind.

His father had lent him a copy of my book, *Ghost Hunter*, and he had looked forward to reading it when exams eased up a bit. But now, even though he was in another room without the slightest trace of a ghost, he could not bring himself to touch my book. Instead, he concentrated all his reading on humorous books.

Unfortunately, nobody did anything about the suicide headmaster. So it must be that he keeps coming back that passage to his old room only to find his body still hanging in the shower of the bathroom.

You might ask, what shill I do if I think I have a ghost in the house? Shall I run? Shall I stay? Do I talk to it or ignore it? Is there a rule book for people having ghosts? Some of the questions I get are like that. Others merely wish to report a case because they feel it is something I might be interested in.

Still others want help: free them from the ghost and vice versa. Some are worried: how much will I charge them for the house-cleaning job? When I explain there is no charge and that I will gladly do it, they are relieved. Because ghostly manifestations often do occur to people with very little money.

But so many people have ghosts—almost as many as have termites, not that there is any connection—that I cannot personally go after each and every case brought to my attention by mail, telephone, telegram, or television.

In the most urgent cases I try to come and help the people involved. Usually I do this in connection with a TV show or lecture at the local university, for *someone* has to pay my expenses. The airlines don't accept ghost money nor do the innkeepers. And thus far I am on my own, financially speaking. No Institute or Research Foundation to take up the slack. For destruction and bombs there is always money, but for research involving the psychic, hardly ever.

Granted I can visit a number of people with haunted-house problems every year, what do the others do whom I can't see myself? Can I send them to a local ghost hunter the way a doctor sends patients to a colleague if he can't or does not wish to treat them?

Even if I could, I wouldn't do it. When they ask for my help, they want my approach, and not someone else's, to their peculiar problems. In this field, every researcher sees things a little differently from the next one. I am probably the only parapsychologist who is unhesitatingly pro-ghost. Some will admit they exist but spend a lot of running time trying to find "alternate" explanations, if they cannot discredit the witnesses.

I have long and for good scientific reasons become convinced that ghosts exist. Ghosts are ghosts. Not hallucinations, necessarily, and not mistakes by casual observers. With that sort of practical base to start from, I go after the cases by concentrating on the situation and problems rather than, as some researchers will do, trying hard to change the basic stories reported to me. I don't work on my witnesses; I've come to help them. To try and shake them with the sophisticated apparatus of a trained parapsychologist is not only unfair, but also foolish. The original reports are straight reports by average people of what has happened in their own environment. If you try to shake their testimony, you may get a different story—but it won't be the truth, necessarily. The more you confuse the witnesses the less they will recall that which is firsthand information.

My job begins when the witnesses have told their story for the first time.

In the majority of cases I have handled, I have found a basis of fact for the "complaint" of a ghostly nature. Once in a while a person may have thought something supernormal when it was not. And on rare occasions I have come across mentally unbalanced people living in a fantasy world of their own. There just aren't that many kooks that want my help: evidently my scientific method, even though I am convinced of the veracity of ghostly phenomena, is not the kind of searchlight they wish to have turned on their strange stories.

What to do until the Ghost Hunter arrives? Relax, if you can. Be a good observer, whether or not you are scared stiff. And remember, please—ghosts are also people.

There but for the grace of God goes someone like yourself.

6

DO ANIMALS SURVIVE DEATH?

When I was a young student I once was offered a scholar-
ship to continue my studies of archaeology at Haverford
College, the famous Quaker school.

Unfortunately I could not take up that offer for I was the
sole support of my parents and we lived in New York City,
where I also held down a job writing and editing a numis-
matic-archaeological magazine.

But I got to know the Friends pretty well and was impressed first of all with their antiwar stand and their sincerity
in all they did.

Yet, there was one point on which I found myself differing
completely with the Quaker point of view. That was the
question of animals. I had always felt that if man had a soul,
surely animals did too, being living creatures as much as
we are.

But the Quakers don't seem to see it that way. Man, to
them, stands apart as a divinely created entity, complete
with spirit or soul and similar to God himself. Animals, on
the other hand, were not immortal, and therefore could be
eaten with impunity. As I had been a vegetarian since age
eleven, I could not accept this doctrine and I still find the
practice of killing animals horrid and unnecessary.

In the years of my search for proof of human survival of

death, the question has often been asked of me, what about animal spirits? Animal ghosts? If my views on animal survival are correct, surely there must be some evidence for their continued existence?

Now I realized that finding animal ghosts would in itself not be as exciting as finding human ghosts with whom one might conceivably converse, but the large number of pet owners and just plain animal lovers among us—fortunately there are many—made this a question also relating to people, and as such I started to accumulate evidence for the continued existence of animals in the world of "the mind."

Shirley Sherad, of Quincy, Massachusetts, had a family dog which died a few years ago at age seventeen and a half, having been with them for sixteen and a half years—a long and close association filled with love. A few weeks after the dog died, Shirley's sister came home one evening and on climbing the stairs had the distinct impression of seeing the dog's plumy white tail whisk around the corner, and out of sight.

She was generally disbelieved, but the following night, when Shirley Sherad went up the stairs about the same time, she also noticed the dog's tail—just that happy, wagging tail! Moreover, the spot that had been the dog's in life felt as if there were still a dog sleeping there. After about a month of this "presence," it faded away.

Charlene Sauter of Wenham, Massachusetts, and her mother frequently saw their favorite puppy after his death, but only from the shoulders down. They heard him walking about the house, and saw him run out of the house toward the grave outside where they had buried his body.

Mrs. Elwood Kruse is a housewife in Burlington, Iowa. Her husband is an electrical engineer and neither of them is a student of occult matters, although Mrs. Kruse has a history of premonitions and similar ESP experiences. She has learned to live with it and, if anything, it has made her even more cautious in accepting unorthodox happenings than if she had no such abilities. She has always loved animals and, having been raised in the country, has always been surrounded by dogs, cats, birds, or fish. Her husband at first had some reservations about having animals in a home, but eventually he gave in and allowed her to get a puppy for their daughters.

It was Christmas, 1964, when she bought an Irish setter puppy and named him Fiaca. The children were elated, and even Mr. Kruse, not overly fond of dogs, came to like the animal.

On December 18, 1965, her husband had to telephone Mrs. Kruse to tell her the sad news. Their dog had been run over by a car and killed instantly. Mrs. Kruse was terribly upset. The Christmas season was at hand and memories of Fiaca's arrival a year before would sadden the holidays. But they accepted and tried to bear up under their loss.

On the day before Christmas, exactly one year to the day of the dog's arrival at the Kruse home, Mrs. Kruse was in the kitchen when suddenly she heard a strange noise at the front door. It sounded like a dog scratching to be let in. At once she thought, oh, Fiaca wants to get into the house—then the chilling thought came to her that this could not very well be since he was dead. So she went to the front door and peeked through the glass, but there was nothing outside that could have made the noise. She returned to her kitchen explaining her experience as due to her missing the dog at this time of year.

The incident slipped her mind until a few days after the holiday. This time she heard the sound very clearly again and knew it was not her imagination playing tricks.

Again she looked out the door and saw nothing special. The house was new; the storm door was made of aluminum, and the noise was that of animal claws raking up and down on the metal, just as Fiaca used to do. There was no tree close enough to have caused the noise with its branches scraping against the door. She told her husband about the second experience but he would not believe her, being a practical man.

The sounds kept coming back, usually in the afternoon. Then one night in the second week of January 1966, it happened again. This time she was not alone but was playing bridge in the living room with her husband and their friends Mr. and Mrs. Marvin Turl. Mr. Turl is a psychology student with an interest in parapsychology.

Mr. Kruse and Susan Turl kept playing, evidently not hearing anything. But Marvin Turl looked up. He too had heard the scratching. He knew nothing at that time of Mrs. Kruse's earlier experiences. But he confirmed that the noise sounded to him like a dog scratching on the door to be let in. Mrs. Kruse and Mr. Turl went to the door and flipped the porch light on. There was no dog outside. Nothing.

The next day Mrs. Kruse confided the strange happenings to her mother and found her receptive to the idea of a psychic phenomenon involving their dog.

She suggested that Mrs. Kruse acknowledge her pet dog's presence verbally the next time the scratching occurred, and open the door as if the dog were actually present.

Two days went by with Mrs. Kruse hoping the ghostly scratching would return. On the third day, in the afternoon, she heard the familiar scratching again. Quickly she went to the door, opened it wide, and said, "Come on in, Fiaca."

She felt terribly silly doing this, but after she had done it, the depression over the dog's untimely death seemed somehow to have left her and she felt better about the whole matter.

She then returned to her kitchen for a while and continued her work. A little later she found herself in the living room.

Imagine her surprise when she found the carpet near the front door covered by a whitish substance, similar to fine dust. The substance trailed into the dining room, where it disappeared for a stretch, only to reappear near the door leading from the kitchen to the living room. She found more of the white substance in the hall, most of it at the end where Fiaca used to curl up on the carpet and sleep. From that spot he could observe all three bedrooms, and it was his favorite spot.

Although Mrs. Kruse had no knowledge of the nature of ectoplasm or materializations, it struck her at once that the white substance marked exactly the way Fiaca used to go about the house: from the front door into the dining room, then a mad dash through the kitchen, and then down the hall to check the bedrooms.

She looked at the white stuff but did not touch it. A little later, her father passed by it and observed it too. But by nightfall it had somehow dissolved.

The scratching at the front door was never heard again after that day.

Perhaps, Mrs. Kruse thinks, the dog wanted to come home one more time to make sure everything was all right.

The Kruses are glad he took the trouble, for they know that Fiaca is all right too, in his new place.

There are reports of wild animals appearing after their deaths, but the majority of incidents concern domestic animals, especially dogs and cats. Perhaps it is because our pets take on part of our human personality and thus rise above the status of "dumb animals," or perhaps because the bond of love is so strong between master and pet.

New Yorker Kirsten Meyer had a curious experience when she lived in a converted loft on West Forty-sixth Street, back in 1959.

Somebody evidently had had a pet cat in the place before she moved in, and the cat had died there. Cats are tied to places rather than people and evidently this cat decided to stay on.

At any rate, Miss Meyer frequently saw this ghost cat in the apartment. At first she did not mind, since spectral animals require no food and leave no residue.

But what unnerved her finally was the time she was vacuuming the place and almost scooped the ghost cat up from her favorite corner.

7

HOW FAR OUT IS FAR OUT?

When you're a Psychic Investigator and constantly before the public via television, radio, and books, you're bound to meet a lot of strange people.

Now some people are strange only in that they have psychic gifts that defy so-called natural explanations. Others, in addition to such gifts, are also strange in their interpretations and attitudes toward the uncanny.

I'm often asked, "I guess you hear from a lot of kooks?"

Strange as it seems, if I may use this often abused term, I don't. To the materialist, anyone with an unorthodox experience is a kook.

When our forefathers chose the American motto, *e pluribus unum,* one out of many, they meant it as a statement of unity. But today's Americans have made conformity their god. Do like the good neighbors do, and you'll be all right. Don't be different. Only kooks are different.

So I don't consider anyone with an exciting though unusual experience a kook merely because we may not be able to fit his experience into the established order of things.

And yet there is that small fringe of people who do worry the sincere parapsychologist. Obviously there must be delusion, fraud, and plain nonsense represented amid the people with psychic experiences. It is present among doctors and lawyers and inventors and businessmen, so why not among psychics and people with psychic experiences?

More often than not, the intent is entirely honorable and not at all meant to "put one over" on anyone, not even oneself. And there is always that small doubt in my mind that the story they tell might just be true and it is I who am the narrow-minded one.

Take the strange case of the bat and the mirror, for instance.

"I'm aggressive, clever, yet sensitive and understanding," writes Mrs. Sophia K., a Boston Greek lady who heard of me through the Bob Kennedy TV show. "All in all I'm a normal human being."

Quite so. Her grandfather was a philosopher, like any good Greek should be, and her husband builds medical instruments at Harvard. The lady herself is a housewife, but— and thereby hangs our tale—she has been active in real estate and has a college education. They have two children, aged twenty and seventeen, and are not at all interested in psychic matters despite that philosopher-grandfather.

The incident that shook poor Mrs. K. to her bones happened on an ordinary night in July of 1963. She was about to retire for the night and transferred a crucifix she wore in her clothes to her nightgown. Her husband was already asleep as were their two sons; the hour was close to midnight and their bedroom was reasonably light due to street lighting coming in through the large window.

As she lay down in bed, she suddenly felt very strange. Her whole body seemed paralyzed, although she could think as clearly as before. At that precise moment she heard a loud flapping of wings on the right side of her head, and turning her eyes she noticed a most peculiar bird.

It was a bat, but had a human body, arms, legs, and a head, but no face—like a mythological or heraldic animal. Mrs. K. says she saw this thing over her head and she was petrified, which I believe, for I would be petrified if an ordinary bat were to appear over my head, let alone a human one.

Apparently the bird did not like the position over Mrs. K.'s head, for it flew against the closed window, hit it with a bang, and then returned, a prisoner trying to get out. At that moment Mrs. K. reports she noticed a luminous light in her hallway on her right. The bat gave a deafening flap of its wings and flew into the dresser mirror, where it disappeared.

At that moment, Mrs. K.'s body relaxed and her paralysis was completely gone.

She woke her husband but he had not heard or felt anything unusual. He assured his beloved wife that she must have been dreaming.

Mrs. K. went to see two priests, for two holy men are better than one, she thought. Both men of the cloth listened to her earnestly, then assured her it was not a dream.

How they could do this, I don't know. But they also warned her that the dresser mirror now contained something unspeakably evil.

Until the mirror is put through a church ritual the bat will be in it, Mrs. K. was told.

Naturally the ritual was expensive, but then, how many bats fly into dresser mirrors?

Symbolic visions, often involving birds, are nothing new. Whether thought forms can indeed materialize into the physical to such an extent that they appear material is one of the borderline questions as yet not fully explored.

David V. is a young man living in Los Angeles, who served a tour of duty in Japan. While still in training at Camp Cooke, California, in 1950, Mr. V. had a most unusual experience. One dark evening toward the end of the year, he was walking down the street of the camp. He and some buddies had been to a movie. Ahead of him about two hundred feet he clearly saw the figure of a skeleton walking!

Since it was not Hallowe'en and Mr. V. was cold sober, this was rather a shock—he could not believe his eyes. Cautiously he glanced around to see if the men walking beside him noticed what he saw. Nobody seemed to be aware of the skeleton, however, so David accelerated his steps to catch up with the apparition, if that is what it was. But he could not get closer and suddenly it disappeared into one of the buildings along the street.

Ever since then the skeleton has puzzled him, for he is not psychic or interested in ESP. To this day he wonders if he had seen a vision symbolic of death for the man who had actually walked ahead of him.

My appearance on Art Linkletter's television program was a magnet for people with weird experiences who wanted to talk to me about them and maybe find an explanation for what had happened to them.

A lady named Lucille Estelle, of Long Beach, California, invited me to see an amateur movie she had taken in New Mexico a few years ago.

Mrs. Estelle had come across a lonely cemetery in the desert of New Mexico. It was fenced in and seemed quite abandoned. But the old gravestones attracted her and she filmed the scene with her 8-mm. camera.

Imagine her surprise when the films came back from the developing laboratory and inside one of the graves there was a lady rocking in a chair.

That at least was the story told by Mrs. Estelle. When I tried to contact her to see this fantastic movie, neither she nor her print could be found and the phone just rang and rang. Perhaps Mrs. Estelle was off again somewhere with her camera, but until I catch up with her we won't know if the lady in the grave is still rocking, or off her rocker by now.

A lady in Detroit wrote to me in great despair after she had read an article of mine in the Detroit *Free Press*. Her "complaint" was the kind you cannot usually discuss over the telephone.

Evidently a psychically sensitive person, she felt herself surrounded by unseen entities. She had tried to get rid of them—since she was not interested in being a medium—only to find them more persistent than ever. (I am withholding her name and address, but I have both.) Gradually the phenomena were accompanied by strange odors, and she felt herself being touched bodily in an unmistakable manner. Her physician sent her to see a psychiatrist. She did not go, considering herself sound in mind and body. Perhaps. But the number of women, generally middle-aged or frustrated, who complain of sexual assault by spirits, is apparently on the increase.

The strange thing about such outlandish claims is that such phenomena are possible. In some cases I have investigated I have come to the conclusion that the victims are telling the truth. By the same token, there are others where we are dealing with a kind of wish fulfillment hysteria.

A young woman in Long Island refused to leave her apartment until I came to see her about the "poltergeist" invading her privacy. She too had shown mediumistic leanings before the incidents began, but her mother's death had apparently touched off some overt acts. The close relationship between mother and daughter gone, the daughter found herself frightened and alone in what was formerly her mother's apartment. As her fears mounted, she would observe faces before her, and she found herself being molested by unknown assailants, especially in the dark of night.

Sometimes the Psychic Investigator must also be a good psychologist.

I went over the young woman's life with her, pinpointed her emotional problems and tried to help her face them.

Gradually fear of the unknown left her and she felt she would be able to cope with the psychic that nature had given her without so much as asking her permission.

Another sincere lady who came to see me to evaluate her automatic writing—the ability to receive controlled messages from discarnate individuals—not only wrote in the name of some recently deceased individuals, but generously included George Washington and Abraham Lincoln.

Again I say that it is entirely conceivable that someone, somewhere, might receive a genuine message from such distinguished sources, but I can only reserve judgment until such writing is found to be full of information unknown to the automatist and yet confirmed independently.

In the "old" days when Mike Douglas did his TV show from Cleveland, there came a day when someone tipped his producer off to my activities. The producer was an imaginative fellow by the name of Rift Fournier. He conceived the notion that I should come to Cleveland and investigate a haunted house for the benefit of the TV audience—and it wasn't even Hallowe'en. That was all right with me, and I politely inquired whether he had any particular haunted house in mind. After all, if I had to furnish my own haunted house I might as well not bother—especially in Cleveland, which is a very unghostly type town. Well, Rift didn't have a ghost to stand on, either, it developed, but he knew a newspaper columnist named George Condon and turned to him for fatherly advice or maybe some free space.

Mr. Condon met the producer at the nearest bar and a spirited conversation ensued, in the course of which he pointed out to Rift that Cleveland had a haunted house all right, yes indeed it had, and he supplied the Mike Douglas braintrust with name and address of the people who had seen the ghost.

He even wrote a column about it, complete with every

ghost cliché in the book. But it was all in good, clean, ghastly fun.

I arrived in Cleveland on September 3, 1963, was whisked to the station not on a broom but by a yellow cab, and given the Big Ghost Hunter treatment. The idea was to go out to the house that night, complete with camera crews and producer. I was doubtful, but I had come a long way, and said, "O.K., I'll try. First, however, let me talk to the people who have seen the ghosts."

This was no problem, and an hour later I met a quiet, dignified middle-class Negro couple by the name of Mr. and Mrs. Thomas Todd. We decided to tape an interview and get to the bottom of the matter, if it had a bottom.

In 1958 the Todds, in the middle twenties, signed a lease for an apartment at what is called Mason Court. This is a block of apartments in a suburb of Cleveland not exactly enjoying the best reputation. On visiting the place for the first time, however, they heard some neighborhood gossip about it being a haunted house, but they put no stock in such talk and signed the lease anyway. A few weeks after they had moved in and settled down in the house, they became increasingly aware that all was not well with their place. The house is a two-story, two-family house, and the bathroom is in the lower portion. Strange noises in the bathroom brought Mr. Todd down to investigate one night. There was a clicking and swishing sound and since Todd knew that the bathroom had to be empty, he was puzzled. Naturally he tried to open the door and was even more puzzled. He couldn't budge it. "Someone is holding that door from inside," he reasoned, but that didn't make any sense either.

He decided to go back upstairs and discuss it with his wife. She didn't believe him, so he went downstairs again and tried the door once more.

This time the door opened immediately when he only touched it lightly. He decided that he had been the victim of his own imagination, and since the noise had stopped also, he went back to bed.

Several days later, the strange noises returned, and this time Mrs. Todd also heard them. What's more, there were clearly footsteps on the ground floor. The couple decided to brave the intruder together. When they reached the ground floor, they were met by a curious sight. Not a burglar, but a whitish hand sticking out of a trap door in one corner of the floor. This trap door led to the cellar, but there was nothing unusual in that cellar, to their knowledge.

Some moonlight filtered in through the windows and they could see the hand clear enough.

Before you could say Ghost Hunter, they were up the stairs and back in bed.

But the phenomena continued to plague them. On one occasion they observed two fingers rise from what they knew was a solid floor. The next day, in the daylight, they investigated their floor inch by inch: no holes or other opening through which fingers could have come up. As if that would have helped their nerves.

At this point they went to the police and as rationally as possible they explained their problem. Naturally the police didn't exactly believe them. But they were willing to come and trap the human joker causing all this trouble. The cop on the beat paid the Todds a visit at their usual "witching hour," which was around 10:30 P.M. He saw the white hand too. When he turned in his report, his superiors thought he had been too long on the force and should be retired quickly, but his record was so good they decided to humor him.

Consequently it was arranged a little later that another officer and a skeptical newspaperman should come for another visit. The Todds by this time were really upset by all these goings-on, and they in turn invited a few friends for moral support, so the downstairs part of their house held exactly thirteen people the night they decided to lay the

Rita Atlanta, exotic dancer, in front of her haunted trailer near Boston.

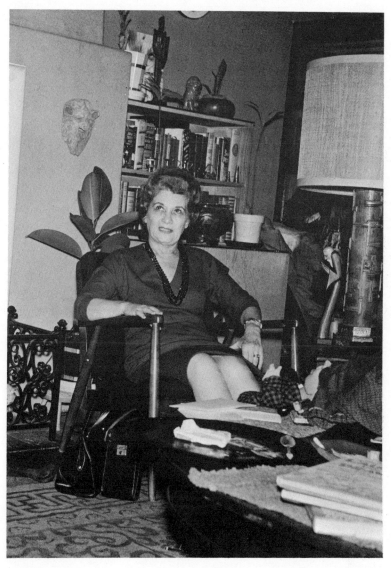

Medium Betty Ritter during clairvoyance at Gay Street, New York, puppet theatre.

Ethel Johnson Myers, trance medium, getting bearings at haunted Jumel Mansion, New York.

Skryne Castle, Ireland, is haunted by the wraith of a young girl murdered by a rejected suiter. Sybil Leek cautiously enters the haunted room.

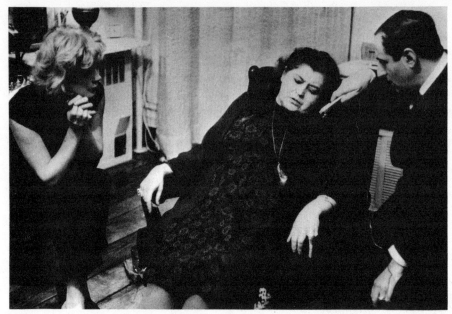

Hans Holzer speaking to "Hungry Lucy," ghost of a 1792 camp follower, through entranced medium Sybil Leek, as actress June Havoc, owner of the house, looks on.

World famous as a haunted house is Ocean-born Mary's at Henniker, New Hampshire, said to be still guarded by original owner, Mary Wallace.

*Cash register on left once flew off counter by own volition
in this psychically active inn at Bath, England.*

*Hans Holzer investigating a haunted church at Millvale, Pennsylvania,
where ghost of a onetime priest has been seen.*

The trap door at Mason Court, Cleveland, where a ghostly white hand was reported sticking out from the floor.

Workroom of Dianne Nicholson's New York apartment, where skeleton-like figure was seen.

Hamburg, Germany, apartment house with owner of disturbed apartment standing on third-floor terrace.

Makeshift grave where skeletons of two people were found buried in Austrian farmhouse.

ghost. Sure enough, there was that hand again, sticking out of the trap door.

The cop shot at it with his revolver, with the bullets going right through the white hand into the trap door. The hand immediately vanished. They turned on all lights and lifted the trap door. Not a trace of anyone under it. No blood. Nothing whatever.

The policeman scratched his head and in a shaky voice suggested that this was a little outside his beat. But he knew a priest who could probably have a go at it, seeing that this was more up his alley. The Todds agreed readily, for all they cared about was to get rid of the phenomenon, not necessarily to find out what caused it.

A priest came and performed the ritual of exorcism. Evidently the ghost was not very religious, for he or she paid absolutely no attention to the ceremony. The visitations continued and it got to be so bad they did not dare come downstairs any more at night. That wasn't what the young couple had bargained for for their first home, however. They notified the owner that they were leaving. To their surprise, there was no objection. So they left.

Much later, the husband had occasion to pass through the area on business. He decided to find out if the new tenants had been any luckier than they had been. It was then that he finally learned why the house had had so many short-term tenants.

A woman neighbor, who remembered Todd, assured him that he had done the smart thing by moving out. Some years ago, there lived in the house a couple who did not get on too well. The husband was unusually jealous of his wife, and once, during a fit of jealousy, he killed her. That at least was the talk of the neighborhood. One could not be sure, for the husband had disappeared since then, and the woman's body was never found. After a while, the owners rented the house again.

So far, so good, I thought. It is a plausible story. The witnesses seem honest and quite sane. It had been five years since the event, and unfortunately they did not recall the names of the police officers, or the newspaperman, or the name of the neighborhood woman who clarified the cause of the haunting for them. I found this puzzling, but Condon—whom I met at a bar nearby to get acquainted and talk ghosts—assured me the case had indeed been in the papers at that time, but even he could not furnish me with names. I only had a few hours in Cleveland, so we decided to go ahead anyway and try to see if the hand would stick out for me that night.

But we did manage to learn the murdered woman's name: Edna.

We arrived at what I can only call a most dilapidated house. Boarded up on all sides, it was obvious at once that the house had been out of use for some time. The area had deteriorated even further since the time the Todds had lived there, and there was an overall stench hanging around the alley that no self-respecting ghost would be able to stomach, I thought. But bravely we went inside. The cameramen put up their equipment, and since no lights were left in the house, we didn't have to turn any out. I had a large flashlight and with that I looked around. There was the trap door all right, leading to the basement.

We didn't have a medium along so I really expected nothing much. But of course some manifestations happen to ordinary people. The Todds had refused to come along, and if any of us had any psychic abilities, they were hiding them well.

Condon lit up the proceedings with his jovial presence, however. After half an hour of shivering in the dark I decided to get the show on the road or quit.

"Edna," I said softly, "I've come to talk to you."

There wasn't a sound. Evidently Edna was not in the

mood. Then, too, the grinding noises of the movie cameras and the constant playing of lights by the crew did not exactly help things any. I realized that the trap had been sprung, but I was in it.

I should have stayed in New York.

Instead of a quiet look at what might or might not be a genuine site of phenomena, it turned out to be a fully covered news conference with Edna, the ghost presumptive. Only Edna didn't show.

I shook my head and hinted that we'd have to come back another time with a psychic.

"Let's look around and then go," I suggested and Condon heartily agreed, for he was getting cold and lonely for his home away from home. I stepped into the next room downstairs and played the flashlight around the floor in routine fashion.

Suddenly the light hit a shapeless form on the floor. There was a heavy, dark blanket there, and underneath the blanket . . . something moved.

Quickly I pulled back the blanket.

Then we all saw it. There was no mistake about it. No, not a ghost. A local bum sleeping off his own encounter with the spirits.

8

THE STRANGE DEATH OF VALERIE K.

Sometimes being a Psychic Investigator puts a heavy moral burden on one, where there may be a possibility of preventing someone's death. Of course, you're never sure that you can. Take the case of Valerie K., for instance. I am not using her full name because the case is far from closed. The police won't talk about it. But her friends are only too sure there is something mysterious about her death, and they will talk about it. Mainly to me, for that's about all they can do about it—now.

To start at the beginning, in April of 1967 I got a phone call from Sheila M.—an English girl whom I had met through a mutual friend—inviting my wife and me to a cocktail party at her house on New York's East Side. Now if it's one thing my wife and I hate it's cocktail parties, even on the East Side, but Sheila is a nice person and we thought she was likely to have only nice friends, so I said yes, we'd come. The party was on April 20, 1967, and when we arrived everybody was already there, drinking and chatting, while the butler passed between the guests ever so quietly seeing after their needs.

Since I don't drink I let my wife talk to Sheila and sauntered over to the hors d'oeuvres, hopefully searching for some cheese bits, for I am a vegetarian and don't touch meat or fish. Next to the buffet table I found not only an empty chair, which was unusual in this crowded apartment right now, but also a lovely young woman in a shiny silver Oriental-style dress. In fact, the young lady was herself an Oriental, a very impressive-looking girl perhaps in her middle twenties, with brown hair, dark eyes, and a very quiet, soigné air about her. It turned out the girl's name was Valerie K., and I had been briefly introduced to her once before on the telephone when Sheila had told her of my interest in psychic research, and she had wanted to tell me of some of her experiences.

We got to talking about our mutual interest in ESP. She sounded far away, as if something were troubling her, but I had the impression she was determined to be gay and not allow it to interfere with her enjoyment of the party. I knew she was Sheila's good friend and would not want to spoil anything for her. But I probed deeper, somehow sensing she needed help. I was right, and she asked me if she could talk to me sometime privately.

There were several eager young men at the party whose eyes were on the lovely Oriental, so I thought it best not to preempt her time, since I knew she was not married. I gave her my telephone number and asked her to call me whenever she wanted to.

About an hour later we left the party and when we got home I suppressed a desire to telephone this girl and see if she was all right. I dismissed my feeling as undue sentimentality, for the girl had seemed radiant, and surely the reason for her wanting to see me would have to be psychic rather than personal in the usual sense.

All through the weekend I could not get her out of my mind, but I was busy with other work and decided to call her first thing the following week.

Monday night, as I read the *Daily News,* my eye fell on a brief article tucked away inside the newspaper, an article telling of the death of two women a few hours before. The paper's date was Tuesday morning. The deaths had occurred early Monday morning. One of the two was Valerie K.

With a shudder I put down the paper and closed my eyes.

Could I have prevented her death? I will let you be the judge. But first let me show you what happened in the final hours of this girl's life on earth. Every word is the truth . . .

Valerie K. came from a well-to-do Chinese family residing in Hawaii. She was as American as anyone else in her speech and yet there was that undefinable quality in the way she put her words together that hinted at Eastern thought. After an unhappy and brief marriage to a Hong Kong business-man, she came to New York City to try her luck on her own. Never particularly close to her parents, she was now entirely on her own and needed a job. She found a job vaguely de-scribed as a public relations assistant, but in fact, she was a secretary to the man who did publicity for the company. But somehow she was not quite right for the job or the job for her and it came to a parting of the ways.

The new girl hired to take her place was Sheila. Despite the fact that the English girl replaced her, they struck up a friendship which developed into a true attachment to each other, so much so that Valerie would confide in Sheila to a greater extent than she would in her own people.

When Valerie left the office, there was no job waiting for her; fortunately, however, she had met the manager of a firm owned by the same company, and the manager, whose initial was G., took her on not entirely for unselfish reasons. He had a sharp eye for beauty and Valerie was something special. Thus she found herself earning considerably more than she would have been paid in any similar job elsewhere. Soon the manager let her know that he liked her and she got to like him, too. Between August and October of 1966, they became close friends.

But in October of that year she called her friend Sheila to

complain bitterly of the humiliation she had been put to. G. had found another girl to take her place. Innocently, the new girl, Lynn, became the pawn in the deadly game between the manager and the Chinese beauty.

G. found fault with her very appearance and everything she did, criticizing her and causing her to lose face—to an Oriental an important matter not easily forgotten.

Still, she cared for the man and hoped that he would resume his former attentions. He didn't, and after a miserable Christmas which she partially shared with Sheila, the axe fell. He fired her and gave her two weeks' pay, wishing her the best.

When Sheila heard about this she suggested that Valerie register at the Unemployment office. Instead, the proud girl took sleeping pills. But she either did not take enough or changed her mind in time, for she was able to telephone Sheila and tell her what she had one. The familiar call for a doctor followed and she was saved. She had a session with a psychiatrist after that and seemed much more cheerful.

But the humiliation and rejection kept boiling within her. Nothing can be as daring as a woman scorned, and one day Valerie wrote a personal letter to the owner of the companies she had once worked for, denouncing the manager and his work.

As if nourished by her hatred, her psychic abilities increased and she found she was able to influence people through telepathy, to read others' thoughts and to put herself into a state of excitement through a form of meditation.

All this of course was for the purpose of getting even not only with the manager but with the world that had so often hurt her.

Nobody knew for sure if she ever got a reply to her letter. But she was a regular at an Oriental restaurant near her apartment and became friendly with the owners. There she talked about her plans and how she would show the world what sort of girl she was.

Meanwhile the manager found himself short of help and asked her back. Despite her deep hatred for the man, she went back, all the time scheming and hoping her fortunes would take a turn for the better. But she did confide in Sheila that she had taken a big gamble and if it worked she'd be all right in more ways than one. The owner of the restaurant saw her on Friday, April 21—a day after the party at which I had met her for the first time—and she seemed unusually happy.

She would marry a prominent European, she told him; she had been asked and would say yes. She was almost obsessed at this point with the desire to tell the whole world she would marry him; her parents in Hawaii received a letter requesting them to have formal Chinese wedding attire made up for her in Paris, because she would marry soon. Had the idea of getting even with G. robbed her of her senses? It is difficult to assess this, as the principals involved quite naturally would not talk and even I prefer that they remain anonymous here.

That weekend—April 22 and 23, 1967—the pitch of her "wedding fever" rose higher and higher. A neighbor who had dropped in on her at her apartment found her clad only in a bikini and drinking heavily. She observed her running back and forth from her telephone, trying to reach the man she said she would marry overseas. But she couldn't get through to him. In the meantime, she started giving possessions away, saying she would not need them any longer now that she would marry so rich a man.

She also drew up a list of all those whom she would help once she had become the wife of the millionaire. The neighbor left rather perturbed by all this, and Valerie stayed alone in her apartment—or did she?

It was 4 A.M. when the police received a call from her telephone. It was a complaint about excessive noise. When an officer—initialed McG.—arrived on the scene at 4:20, Valerie herself opened the door in the nude.

"Go away," she said, and asked to be left alone. The officer quickly surveyed the scene. She became rude and explained she was expecting a phone call and did not wish to be disturbed. The officer reported that she had been alone and was drinking, and there the matter stood.

The minutes ticked away. It was early Monday morning, April 24, 1967.

At precisely 5 A.M., the building superintendent looked out his window and to his horror saw something heavy fall on his terrace.

Rushing to the scene, he discovered Valerie's broken body. She had been killed instantly. The girl had taken two roses with her—but one somehow remained behind on the window sill of the open window from which she had plunged to her death. The other sadly fluttered to earth even as she did.

The police officers found themselves back at the apartment sooner than they had expected, only this time there was a cause for action. After a routine inspection of the girl's tenth floor apartment, her death was put down to accidental death or suicide by falling or jumping from her window. Since she had been drinking heavily, they were not sure which.

Monday night Sheila called me frantically, wondering what she should do. There was no one to claim the girl's body. Neither her sister Ethel nor her parents in Hawaii could be reached. I told her to calm down and keep trying, meanwhile berating myself for not having called Valerie in time to prevent her death.

Eventually the parents were found and a proper funeral arranged.

But the puzzle remained. Had she committed suicide or not?

Did that call from Europe finally come and was it so humiliating that Valerie could no longer face the world? Was there not going to be a wedding after all—then at least a funeral?

Valerie had been particularly fond of two things in life—flowers and jewelry. To her, losing a favorite piece of jewelry was bad luck.

Lynn, the girl who now worked at Valerie's office, is a rather matter-of-fact person not given to emotional scenes or superstitions.

Valerie owned a pair of earrings made of jade which G. had had made for her in the days when they were close. About a month before her death, Valerie gave those earrings to Lynn as a gift. There was a special stipulation, however. She must not wear them around the office, since people had seen Valerie wear them and presumably knew their history.

Lynn agreed not to wear them around the office, but when she wore them outside a most unusual phenomenon took place. Suddenly the earrings would not stay put. One and then the other would drop off her ears as if pulled by some unseen force. That was on April 13 and Valerie was still alive, though she had seemed very distraught.

Word of Lynn's concern with the falling earrings got back to the former owner and finally Valerie called to assure her the falling was a "good omen." Then, a week later, on Saturday, April 22, she suddenly called Lynn shortly before midnight, asked her to wear "her" earrings at the office. Lynn promised she would wear them to work on Monday.

That was the day Valerie died. The following day, still wearing the earrings, which seemed now to cling properly to her ears, she found herself in the ladies' room, when she felt her right earring whipped off by force and thrown into the toilet. It felt as if it had been snatched from her ear.

Returning to her desk, she noticed that an unusual chill pervaded the area where Valerie's desk had stood. It disappeared at 4:30, which was the time Valerie usually left for home.

All this proved too much for Lynn and she went on a week's vacation.

Sheila was still very upset when a male friend dropped in to help her in this sorry matter. The gentleman, a lawyer by profession, had taken off his jacket when he suddenly felt a cuff link leave his shirt. It was a particularly intricate piece of jewelry and no matter how they searched it was never found again.

Was the dead girl trying to show her hand? Too phantastic, and yet . . .

There was no rational explanation for the sudden disappearance, in plain light and in the presence of two people, of so definite an object as a cuff link.

On Friday of that week, after the girl had been buried, her sister, Ethel, who had finally arrived in town, went to the apartment to find out what she could about her sister's effects.

As soon as she entered the apartment she realized that a terrific fight had taken place in it. Nothing had been touched from the moment of death until her arrival, as the apartment had been sealed. Three knives were lying on the floor and the place was a shambles. On the table she noticed two glasses, one still partially filled with Scotch and one almost empty. When she called the police to report the strange appearance of the place she was given the cold shoulder.

Who was the person Valerie had entertained during her last hours on earth?

The superintendent reported to the sister that Valerie had received two letters since her death, but when they looked at the mailbox, it was empty.

A friend, the owner of the restaurant Valerie had frequented, notified the telephone company to cut off service and forward the final bill to her. She was told the bill could not be found.

And so it went. Was someone covering up his traces? Sheila heard these things and went to work. To her, something was terribly wrong about her friend's death and she was going to find out what. Questioning both the restaurant owner and the girl's sister again, she came upon another strange fact. The ash trays Ethel had found in the apartment had two different types of cigarets in them—L & M and Winston. Valerie always smoked L & M. Who smoked Winston?

The police seem not particularly interested in pursuing the matter. They think it was Valerie herself who called them the first time, and that she just decided to end it all in a drunken stupor. That at least is the impression they gave Sheila.

The following day, Saturday, the window was still open. The rose Valerie had left behind was still on the sill, despite the windy weather of April.

That night, when Sheila was putting on her jacket, she felt somebody helping her into it. She was alone, or so she thought.

It occurred to her then that Valerie's spirit was not at rest and could I please help? The very least I could do was talk to her *now*, since fate had prevented me from getting to her in time.

I arranged with Betty Ritter to be ready for me the following weekend, without telling her where we would be going, of course. The date was May 6, 1967, the time 3 P.M., and Sheila was to meet us at the apartment that once belonged to Valerie, but now was cleaned out and empty—ready for the next occupant. The superintendent agreed to let us in, perhaps sensing why we had come or not caring. At any rate he opened the tenth floor apartment for us and left us alone inside.

As we reached the elevator of the East Sixty-third Street building, Betty Ritter suddenly remarked that she felt death around her. I nodded and we went upstairs.

As soon as we had stepped through the door into Valerie's place, Betty became a psychic bloodhound. Making straight for the window—now closed—she touched it and withdrew in horror, then turned around and looked at me.

"There is a man here jumping around like mad," she said, "but there is also someone else here—I am impressed with the initial E." She then took off her coat and started to walk toward the bathroom. There she stopped and looked back at me.

"I hear a woman screaming . . . I saw blood . . . now I see the initial M . . . she was harmed . . . it is like suicide . . . as if she couldn't take it any more."

Betty had difficulty holding back her emotions and was breathing heavily.

"She left *two* behind," she said. "I see the initials L. and S."

Betty Ritter, not a trance medium but essentially a clairvoyante, is very strong on initials, names, letters, and other forms of identification and she would naturally work that way even in this case.

"I heard her say, 'Mama, Mama'—she is very agitated.

"I also get a man's spirit here . . . initial J."

"How did this girl die?" I interjected at this point.

"She couldn't take it any more. She shows the initial R. This is a living person. She gulped something, I think."

I thought that Betty was picking up past impressions now and wanted to get her away from that area into the current layer of imprints.

"How exactly did she die?" I queried the medium. Betty had no idea where she was or why I had brought her here.

"I think she tried . . . pills . . . blood . . . one way or the other . . . in the past. She was a little afraid but she did plan this. She is very disturbed now and she does not know how to get out of this apartment. I get the initial G. with her."

I asked Betty to convey our sympathies to her and ask her if there was something she wished us to do.

While Betty talked to the spirit girl in a low voice, I reflected on her evidence so far. The initials given—E. was the first initial of Valerie's sister's name, Ethel, M. was Mary, her mother, and G. the manager of the company with whom she had had a relationship—it all seemed to make sense. Betty Ritter had also correctly "gotten" the attempted suicide by pills and pointed out the window as a "hot" area.

What was to follow now?

"She is crying," Betty reported. "She wants her loved ones to know that she didn't mean it. She shows me the head of an Indian and it is a symbol of a car—a brand name I think —it's red—the initial H. comes with this and then she shows me writing, something she has left unfinished. She asks her mother to forgive her because she could not help herself."

I decided to ask Valerie some important questions through the medium. Was she alone at the time of her death?

"Not alone. Initial A. A man, I feel him walking out of the door. Agitating her, agitating her."

"Was he with her when she died or did he leave before?"

"She says, 'I slammed the door on him.' And then she says, 'And then I did it.'"

"Why?"

"I had gone completely out of my mind . . . could not think straight . . . he drove me to it . . ."

"This man is a living person?"

"Yes."

"Is he aware of what happened to her?"

"Yes."

"Did she know him well?"

"Yes, definitely."

"What was his connection with her?"

Betty was herself pretty agitated now, and, in psychic parlance, she was really hot.

"I see a bag of money," she reported, "and the letters M. or W."

I handed her some personal belongings of Valerie's, brought to the scene in a shopping bag by Sheila and now placed on the stove for Betty to touch. She first took up a pendant—costume jewelry—and immediately felt the owner's vibrations.

"How I loved this," she mumbled. "I see D. R., Doctor . . . this was given to her and there is much love here in connection with this . . . this goes way back . . ."

Somehow the personalities of Betty Ritter and Valerie K. melted into one now and Betty, not quite herself, seemed not to listen any more to my queries, but instead kept talking as if she were Valerie, yet with Betty's own voice, and intonation.

"There's so much I wanted to say and I couldn't at the time . . ."

Now returning to herself again, she spoke of a man in spirit, who was very agitated and who had possessed the girl, not a ghost but someone who had died . . . an older man who had a link with here in the past. J. W. Dark-skinned, but not Negro—India or that part of the world."

It struck me suddenly that she might be talking of Valerie's late husband, the man she had married long ago in Hong Kong; he was much older than she was at the time.

"I have a feeling of falling," Betty suddenly said, "I don't know why. May have something to do with her."

I decided to let her walk around the entire apartment and to try to pick up "hot" areas. She immediately went for the lefthand window.

"Something terrible happened here . . . this is the room . . . right here . . . stronger here . . ."

"Is there another woman involved in this story?" I asked.

"I see the initial M." Betty replied, "and she is with a man who is living, and there is also some jealousy regarding a woman's boy friend . . . she could not take it."

I decided to start the exorcism immediately.

"It's such a short time ago that she went," Betty remarked. "She wants to greet Mary . . . or Marie . . . and an L. To tell L. she is relieved now. Just carry on as usual."

L. was the initial of Lynn, the girl at the office, who had encountered the strange happenings with the earrings.

I decided to test this connection.

"Did she communicate with L. in any way?" I asked.

"Yes," Betty nodded, "I see her by L.'s bed . . . perhaps she frightened her . . . but now she knows . . . didn't mean to frighten her . . . she is leaving now, never wants to get back again . . ."

We were quiet for a moment.

"She's throwing us kisses now," Betty added.

"She would do that," Sheila confirmed, "that was the way she would do it."

And that was that.

Betty lit a cigaret and relaxed, still visibly shaken by the communications for which she had been the carrier.

We put Valerie's pitiful belongings back into the paper bag and left the apartment, which now looked shiny and new, having been given a hasty coat of paint to make it ready for the next occupant.

No further snatching of jewelry from anyone's ears occurred after that and even Sheila, my friend, was no longer trying to reopen the case despite her belief that there was more to it that met the eyes of the police.

We decided to allow Valerie a peaceful transition and not

to stir up old wounds which a reopening of the case would undoubtedly do.

But somehow I can't quite bring myself to forget a scene, a scene I only "saw" through the eyes of a laconic police detective making a routine report: the tall, lovely Oriental girl, intoxicated and nude, slamming the door on the police . . . and two liquor glasses on her table.

Who was that other glass for . . . and who smoked the second cigaret, the brand Valerie never smoked?

Who, then, was the man who left her to die?

9

ONE LAST RIDE

Coronado Beach is a pleasant seaside resort in southern California not far from San Diego. You get there by ferry from the mainland and the ride itself is worth the trip. It takes about fifteen minutes and then you continue by car or on foot into a town of small homes, none grand, none ugly—but pleasant and bathed by the warm California sunshine, vigorously battered on the oceanside by the Pacific, and becalmed on the inside of the lagoon by a narrow body of water.

The big thing in Coronado Beach is the U. S. Navy; either you're in it and are stationed here or you work for them in one way or another: directly, as a civilian, or indirectly by making a living through the people who do work for the Navy and who make their homes here.

Mrs. Francis Jones is the wife of an advertising manager for a Sidney, Ohio, newspaper, who had returned to Coronado after many years in the Midwest. She is a young woman with a college background, above-average intelligence, and of mixed Anglo-Saxon and Austrian background. Her father died a Navy hero testing a dive bomber in 1939 making her mother an early widow.

Gloria Jones married fairly young, and when her husband took a job as advertising manager in Sidney, Ohio, she went right along with him. After some years the job became less attractive, and the Joneses moved right back to Coronado where Jones took up work for the Navy.

They have a thirteen-year-old daughter, Vicki, and live a happy, well-adjusted life; Mr. Jones collects coins and Mrs. Jones likes to decorate their brick house set down in a garden filled with colorful flowers.

In January of 1967 Mrs. Jones sought me out to help her understand a series of most unusual events that had taken place in her otherwise placid life. Except for an occasional true dream, she had not had any contact with the psychic and evinced no interest whatever in it until the events that so disturbed her tranquility had come to pass. Even the time she saw her late father in a white, misty cloud might have been a dream. She was only ten years old at the time and preferred later to think it was a dream. But the experiences she came to see me about were not in that category. Moreover, her husband and a friend were present when some of the extraordinary happenings took place.

Kathleen Duffy was the daughter of a man working for the Convair company. He was a widower and Kathleen was the apple of his eye. Unfortunately the apple was a bit rotten in spots. Kathleen was a most difficult child. Her father had sent her to a Catholic school for girls in Oceanside but she ran away twice, and after the second time she had to be sent to a home for "difficult" children.

Gloria Jones met Kathleen when both were in their teens. Her mother was a widow and Mr. Duffy was a widower, so the parents had certain things in common. The two girls struck up a close friendship and they both hoped they might become sisters through the remarriage of their parents, but it did not happen.

When Kathleen was sent away to the Anthony Home, a reform school at San Diego, Gloria was genuinely sorry. That was in 1951 and Kathleen was about sixteen years of age then. Although they never met again, Kathleen phoned Gloria a few times. She wasn't happy in her new environment, of course, but there was little that either girl could do about it.

In mounting despair, Kathleen tried to get away again but did not succeed. Then one day she and her roommate, June Robeson, decided to do something drastic to call attention to their dissatisfied state. They set fire to their room in the hope that they might escape in the confusion of the fire.

As the smoke of the burning beds started to billow heavier and heavier, they became frightened. Their room was being kept locked at all times. Now they started to bang at the door, demanding to be let out.

The matron came and surveyed the scene. The girls had been trouble for her all along. She decided to teach them what she thought would be an unforgettable "lesson." It was. When Kathleen collapsed from smoke poisoning, the matron finally opened the door. The Robeson girl was saved, but Kathleen Duffy died the next day in the hospital.

When the matter became public knowledge, the local newspapers demanded an investigation of the Anthony Home. The matron and the manager of the Home didn't wait for it. They fled to Mexico and have never been heard from since.

That was in January of 1952 and Gloria gradually began to forget the tragedy.

Two years went by and the image of the girl friend receded into her memory.

One day she and another friend, a girl named Jackie Sudduth, were standing near the waterfront at Coronado, a sunny, wind-swept road whence you can look out onto the Pacific, or back toward the orderly rows of houses that are Coronado Beach.

The cars were whizzing by as the two girls stood idly gazing across the road. One of the cars coming into view was driven by a young man with a young girl next to him who seemed familiar to Gloria. She only saw her from the shoulders up, but as the car passed close by she knew it was Kathleen. Flabbergasted, she watched the car disappear.

"Did you know that girl?" her friend Jackie inquired.

"No, why?"

"She said your name," her friend reported.

Gloria nodded in silence. She had seen it too. Without uttering a sound, the girl in the passing car had spelled the syllables "Glo-ri-a" with her lips.

For weeks afterward, Gloria could not get the incident out of her mind. There wasn't any rational explanation and yet how could it be? Kathleen had been dead since 1951 and this was 1953.

The years went by. Then a strange incident brought the whole matter back into her consciousness. It was New Year's Eve, 1965. She was now a married woman with a daughter. As she entered her kitchen, she froze in her tracks: a bowl was spinning counterclockwise while moving through the kitchen by its own volition.

She called out to her husband and daughter to come quickly. Her daughter's girl friend, Sheryl Konz, age thirteen, was first to arrive in the kitchen. She also saw the bowl spinning. By the time Mr. Jones arrived it had stopped its most unusual behavior.

Over dinner, topic A was the self-propelled bowl. More to tease her family than out of conviction, Mrs. Jones found herself saying, "If there is anyone here, let the candle go out." Promptly the candle went out.

There was silence after that, for no current of air was present that could have accounted for the sudden extinguishing of the candle.

In the summer of 1966 Mrs. Jones was making chocolate pudding in her kitchen. When she poured it into one of three bowls, the bowl began to turn—by itself. This time her husband saw it too. He explained it as vibrations from a train or a washing machine next door. But why did the other two bowls not move also?

Finally wondering if her late friend Kathleen, who had always been a prankster, might not be the cause of this, she waited for the next blow.

On New Year's Day, 1967, she took a Coke bottle out of her refrigerator, also in the kitchen, of course, and set it down on the counter. Then she turned her back on it and went back to the refrigerator for some ice. This took only a few moments. When she got back to the counter, the Coke bottle had disappeared.

Chiding herself for being absent-minded, she assumed she had taken the bottle with her to the refrigerator and had left it inside. She checked and there was no Coke.

Am I going out of my mind? she thought, and picked up the Coke carton. It contained five bottles. The sixth bottle was never found.

Since these latter incidents took place during the three years when they lived in Sidney, Ohio, it was evident that the frisky spirit of Kathleen Duffy could visit them any place they went—if that is who it was.

In late May 1967, back again in Coronado, both Mr. and Mrs. Jones saw the bread jump out of the breadbox before their very eyes. They had locked the breadbox after placing a loaf of bread inside. A moment later, they returned to the breadbox and found it open. While they were still wondering how this could be, the bread jumped out.

A practical man, Mr. Jones immediately wondered if they were having an earthquake. They weren't. Moreover, it appeared that their neighbors' breadboxes behaved normally.

They shook their heads once more. But this time Mrs. Jones dropped me a letter.

On June 3, 1967, I went to San Diego to see the Joneses. Sybil Leek and I braved the bus ride from Santa Ana on a hot day, but the Joneses picked us up at the bus terminal and drove us to the Anthony Home where Kathleen had died so tragically.

Naturally Sybil was mystified about all this, unless her ESP told her why we had come here. Consciously she knew nothing.

When we stopped at the Home we found it boarded up and not a soul in sight. The day was sunny and warm and the peaceful atmosphere belied the past which was probably filled with unhappy memories. After the unpleasant events of 1951, the place had been turned into a school for retarded children and run as such for a number of years, but at present it stood abandoned.

Sybil walked around the grounds quietly and soaked up the mood of the place.

"I heard something, maybe a name," she suddenly said. "It sounds like Low Mass."

Beyond that, she felt nothing at the spot of Kathleen's unhappy memories. Was it Kathleen who asked for a Low Mass to be said for her? Raised a strict Catholic, such a thought would not be alien to her.

"The place we just left," Sybil said as we drove off, "has a feeling of sickness to it—like a place for sick people, but not a hospital."

Finally we arrived at the corner of Ocean Avenue and Lomar Drive in Coronado where Gloria Jones had seen the car with Kathleen in it. All through the trip, on the ferry, and down again into Coronado Island, we avoided the subject at hand.

But now we had arrived and it was time to find out if Sybil felt anything still hanging on in this spot.

"I feel a sense of death," she said slowly, uncertainly. "Despite the sunshine, this is a place of death." It wasn't that there was a presence here, she explained, but rather that someone had come here to wait for another person. The noise around us—it was Sunday—did not help her concentration.

"It's a foreign face I see," Sybil continued. "Someone—a man, with very little hair—who is alien to this place. I see an iris next to his face."

Was the man using the symbol to convey the word Irish perhaps? Was he an ancestor of Kathleen's from over there?

I turned to Mrs. Jones.

"I think what you have witnessed here was the superimposition on a pair of motorists of the spirit image of your late friend. These things are called transfigurations. I am sure if the car had stopped you would have found a stranger in it. Kathleen used her so that you could see her familiar face, I think."

Perhaps Kathleen Duffy wanted to take one more ride, a joy ride in freedom, and, proud of her accomplishment, had wanted her best friend to see her taking it.

There have been no further disturbances or prankish happenings at the Jones house since.

10

THE SKELETON IN THE BED AND OTHER INCREDIBLE BUT TRUE EVENTS

"My friend says this skeleton tried to get into bed with her," my friend Elizabeth Byrd said with conviction and looked at me straight, to see how I would react. I did not disappoint her. I shook my head with determination and informed her somewhat haughtily that skeletons do not get into people's beds, in fact, skeletons don't do much really except maybe on Hallowe'en when there's kids inside them.

But Elizabeth is as good a researcher as she is an author—*Immortal Queen* and *Flowers of the Forest* are among her historical novels—and she insisted that this was not some sort of Hallowe'en prank.

More to please her than out of curiosity, I decided to look into this weird tale. I never take stock in anything that I don't hear firsthand, so I called on Elizabeth's friend to hear all about this skeleton myself. I was prepared for a charming, talky, and garrulous spinster whose imagination was running away with her.

The name on the door read Dianne Nicholson, and it was one of those grimy walk-ups on New York's middle East Side that are slowly but surely turning into slums. Downstairs there was a gun shop and the house was squeezed in between a row of other nondescript houses. Children, none of them particularly tidy-looking, were playing in the street, and trucks lumbered by me on Second Avenue creating a steady din that must have been unnerving to any resident of this building. There were perhaps a dozen names on the board downstairs and an Italian grocery across the street. All in all, it was what New Yorkers call a "neighborhood" without distinction, without much hope for improvement, and without many attractive people.

I pressed the bell and when the buzzer responded, I walked up a flight of stairs, where I found the entrance door to the apartment in the front part of the building slightly ajar.

I stepped inside and closed the door behind me.

"Miss Nicholson?" I said tentatively.

"Coming," a bell-like young voice came from the back of the dimly lit apartment.

As my eyes got used to the place I distinguished that it consisted of a longish foyer, from which doors led to a kitchen, another room, and a small room, reading right to left. It was jumble-full of furniture and things and a glance into the small room on my left showed stacks of papers, a drawing board, and other graphic art paraphernalia strewn about.

My investigation was interrupted by the arrival of Miss Nicholson. It was clear immediately that my image of her had been wrong. An ash blonde of perhaps twenty-two or three, she was slight and erect and looked very determined as she greeted me from the other room in center.

"I'm so glad you came," she began and led me to the couch along the wall of the foyer. "This thing has been getting out of hand lately."

I held up my hand—for I did not want to lose a word of her account. Within a minute, my tape recorder was purring away and the story unfolded.

Dianne Nicholson came to New York from her native Atlanta in the middle of 1964. By training she was a writer, or more specifically, a writer of publicity, advertising, and promotional material, and she was presently working with an advertising agency in Manhattan. She was much too busy with the task, first, of looking for a job, and then of maintaining it, to pay much attention to the house and the little apartment in it that she had rented.

It was inexpensive and within her budget, she did not have to share it with a roommate, and that was what she had wanted. If it was no luxury building, well, it was also convenient to her place of work and she had no complaints.

In addition, she did a lot of extra work at home, free-lance accounts, to better her income, so she was rather absorbed in her professional activities most of the time, seldom allowing herself the luxury of aimless dreaming. Her social life was pleasant, but underneath it all ran a very practical streak, for Dianne had come to New York to make good as a career girl, and work was her way of getting there.

She knew few if any of her neighbors, most of whom were not in her social or professional strata to begin with. But she did manage to strike up a friendship with the girl who had an apartment a few stories above hers. This was a rather buxom German girl in her early thirties who went by the single name of Karina. An artist specializing in small drawings, cards, and other objects on the borderline between art and craft, Karina went around her place most of the time wearing miniskirts when miniskirts had not yet been invented. Her life was lived mainly on the inside of herself and she was happy to pursue this kind of career. Evidently she had left behind her in Germany a far different life, but there were no regrets. The two girls visited each other frequently, and it made both of them feel safe to know either one of them was not entirely alone in this dank building.

It was in the middle of 1965, after living in the building for about a year, that Dianne became alarmed by a sequence of events she could not cope with.

At the time, she slept in the smaller room, off the foyer, which later became her workroom.

She awoke there one night and saw a figure standing at her door. It was a rather tall woman, wearing what to Dianne looked like a long nightgown. The figure also wore a kind of Mother Hubbard cap, like a granny would—and yet, Dianne quickly realized that this was not an old figure at all.

As Dianne, with curiosity at first, and increasing terror later, sat up in bed and studied the apparition, she noticed that the figure was luminescent and emitted a soft, white glow. The face, or rather the area where the facial characteristics should be, was also aglow, but she could not make out any features. As yet unsure as to what the figure was, Dianne noticed she could not distinguish any hands either.

At this moment the figure left the spot at the door and got into bed with her.

Dianne's first impression, when the figure got close, was that of a skeleton, but when it got into bed with her she realized that it was more of a waxen figure, very cold but as hard as flesh would be.

Her thoughts racing through her mind while practically paralyzed by the whole thing, Dianne tried to reason it out. Then she said to herself, why, it must be my mother. What in the world would come into bed with her?

Later, she realized that it wasn't her mother, of course. But at the moment she preferred to think so, recalling how her mother had often crawled into bed with her when she was a child. And yet she knew at this moment, crystal clear, that the white figure next to her was that of a young woman.

Touching the figure, she felt hard substance underneath the gown.

"I must see your face," she mumbled and tried to see the stranger's face. But the figure acted as if she were asleep and did not wish to be disturbed.

Dianne reached out and pulled the covers off the bed. She found herself staring into a mirror. Now she realized why she had not been able to see the creature's hands before. They weren't really hands at all, but were more like a skeleton's bony fingers, holding up a mirror in front of the figure's face.

Then the mirror moved and disclosed what took the place of a face: a glowing white round in which neither eyes, nose, nor teeth could be distinguished and yet the whole figure was more than a mere anatomical skeleton—it was a roughly covered skeleton figure—more than mere bones and not quite flesh and skin, but somewhere in between.

Dianne's normal reactions finally caught up with her: she found herself sinking into a slow state of shock at what she had discovered. At this moment, the figure disappeared. Not by retreating to the doorway from where it had come, but just by dissolving from the bed itself.

Dianne leaped out of bed, threw on a robe and raced upstairs to her friend's apartment. For days after, she trembled at the thought of the unspeakable one returning, and she tried hard to convince herself that she had dreamed the whole incident. But in her heart she knew she had not.

From that day on, however, she became increasingly aware of a human presence other than her own in the apartment. More from self-preservation through knowledge than from idle curiosity she bought some books dealing with psychic phenomena.

Early in December this oppressive feeling became suddenly very strong. She had moved her bed into the other bedroom, with a wall separating the two areas. One night she *knew* that an attack had been made upon her and that the evil personality involved was male. She slept with all the lights on from that moment. With mounting terror she would not go off to sleep until daylight reassured her that no further dangers were about.

Then in early January of 1966, just before I came to see her, Dianne had another visit from a white, luminous figure. It was evening, and Dianne had just gotten to sleep. Suddenly she awoke, prodded by some inborn warning system, and there in the entrance to her present bedroom stood a vague, smoke-like figure of some luminescence. After a moment it was gone, only to return again later that same night. Dianne was not alone that night, but it did not help her fears. What did the figure want of her? This was not the skeletal visitor from before but a definitely masculine personality. Dianne knew this entity was after her, and wanted to take her over. On one occasion in December she had felt him take over her nervous system, as she sat helplessly on her bed. Her muscles went into spasm as if they were no longer under her conscious control. Desperately she fought the invader, trying to keep her thoughts on an even keel, and ultimately she won out. The strange feeling left her body and she was able to relax at last.

Extrasensory experiences had plagued Dianne since childhood. When she was fourteen and going to high school, a close friend and sorority sister wrote to her with a strange request. Would she sing at her funeral? Now Dianne had been singing in choir and her friend knew this. But there was no logical reason for so strange a request from a fifteen-year-old girl. Three days after receiving the letter Dianne had a strange dream, in which she saw her friend in front of a large crowd, with her arms wide open, and calling out to Dianne, "Please help me!"

At this point, the dream faded out. She woke up after the dream and noticed that the clock showed 12:45 A.M., Friday.

Sunday night, the identical dream returned, only this time it ended abruptly rather than gently fading out. She discussed the dreams with her classmates in school but could not puzzle out the meaning. On Tuesday she received a phone call from her mother, informing her that her friend had been in an automobile accident on Friday, and at the time of Dianne's first dream the friend had just gone under the anaesthetic at the hospital. At the time of the second dream, which ended abruptly, the girl died.

There were other instances of premonitions come true, of feelings about events that later transpired—making Dianne aware of the fact that she had something special, yet in no way intruding on her practical approach to life.

When she first moved into her present apartment, she found that most of the buildings in the area were occupied by people on welfare relief. But the house she moved into had recently been renovated, making it suitable for higher-rent tenants, as had two others nearby, giving hope that the entire neighborhood might eventually adopt a different image.

Although one of Dianne's boy friends, a photographer, felt nothing special about the apartment, two of her female friends did. There was Karina, the artist upstairs, for instance. She would not stay long, complaining the place gave her the creeps. Elizabeth Byrd also felt an oppressiveness not borne out by the decor or furniture of the place, for Dianne had managed to make the place comfortable and pleasant as far as the purely physical aspects were concerned.

After a while she quit her Madison Avenue job and became a free-lance. This necessitated her spending much more time at home. In the daytime, she found the place peaceful and quiet and she managed to get her work done without trouble.

But as soon as the shadows of night crept over the horizon,

fear began to return to her heart. The fear was not borne from darkness or from the presence of the unknown; it was almost a physical thing with her, something very tangible that seemed to fill a space within the walls of her apartment.

Dianne thought herself safe from the specter in the daytime until one morning she was awakened by a strange noise. She had gone to bed late after putting in long hours of work, and slept until 10 A.M. The noise, she soon realized, was caused by a wooden coat hanger banging heavily against the bedroom door. Still half-asleep, Dianne assured herself that the draft was causing it. She got out of bed, fully awake now, and walked toward the door. The noise stopped abruptly. She checked the door and windows and found everything closed. There could not have been a draft. Still unconvinced, she huffed and puffed to see if her breath would move the hanger. It didn't.

She began to have some strange dreams, several similar ones in succession. In these dreams the skeleton-faced white woman appeared to her and wanted to take her with her.

As the weeks rolled by, more and more strange incidents tried her patience sorely. There was the time she had gone to sleep with all lights burning, when she saw an explosion of light in the living room. It was not hallucinatory, for she saw it reflected in the dark tube of her television set. Another time she was in the bedroom when she heard the sound of glass breaking in the living room. The lights in the living room and the kitchen went out at the same moment. She entered the living room, expecting to see the remnants of a bulb that might have blown up, but there was nothing on the floor. The light switches, however, in both living room and kitchen had been switched off by unseen hands . . . At this moment her friend Karina came down from upstairs and Dianne was never so glad in her life to see a friendly human face.

Since Dianne Nicholson had gotten to be quite frantic

about all this I decided to arrange for a seance to get to the bottom of the disturbances with the help of a good medium. We agreed on June 17, 1966, as the date, Sybil Leek was to be my medium, and Theo Wilson, a reporter from the *Daily News* would come along to witness and report on the investigation.

Meanwhile, Karina, the girl upstairs, had also had her share of run-ins with the Uninvited. Her apartment is on the fifth floor. One day Karina was standing in front of her mirror when she noticed a ghostly figure—or rather a glowing outline. At the same time she felt a strong urge to cut her hair short and be like the apparition. She felt the ghostly presence wanted to possess her or express itself through her and she became frightened. A little later she was down on the second floor with Dianne, when both girls heard a sharp banging noise, as if someone had dumped a heavy object on the floor next to the entrance of the apartment. Their first impression was that a package had been delivered and they rushed to see what it was. But there was nothing there.

When the seventeenth of June arrived it turned out to be one of those oppressive, prematurely hot nights New York is famous for, or rather infamous for, but the date had been set and everyone was in readiness. I also brought along a motion picture camera and on arrival had deposited Sybil with Karina so that I might discuss the events leading up to the investigation once more for the benefit of Theo Wilson of the *News*. Naturally Sybil was not to hear any of this nor was Karina allowed to discuss anything with her temporary guest but the weather—at the moment a most timely subject.

Half an hour later I brought Sybil inside the second floor apartment. Did she feel anything here clairvoyantly?

"You'll probably laugh at this," Sybil said, "but I have a tremendous feeling about horses."

I didn't laugh, and even though I knew of Sybil's love for

and interest in domestic animals, I noted the statement for later verification.

"What about people, though?" I pressed. A heavy oak chair had been placed near the entrance to the smaller room where Dianne had experienced the skeletal intruder originally. The chair was meant for Sybil to sit in and faced away from the small room.

"Behind this chair," Sybil now said, "there is a touch of coldness . . . some nonphysical being, definitely."

The feeling was only fleeting, her main sensation being of a country place with horses, and then that touch of "someone."

I decided to place Sybil into trance now and we—meaning our hostess Dianne Nicholson, a gentleman friend of hers, Karina, Theo Wilson, and myself—grouped ourselves around her. Sybil took the chair facing away from the little room.

After a few moments, heavy, labored breathing replaced the measured breath of Sybil's normal personality. Words came across her lips that I could not yet make out, gradually becoming louder and firmer. I kept asking for a name—asking that the presence identify itself. Eventually the name was clear.

"Jeremy Waters," Sybil had said.

"Speak louder," I commanded.

"Go away," the voice countered, and added, "Jeremy."

"Why should Jeremy go away?"

"Why did he do it . . . nice stock . . . I'm hurt . . . Jeremy, Jeremy Waters . . ."

"Who are you?"

"Waters."

"Who is Jeremy?"

"Jeremy Waters, my son . . . I'll find him . . . ran away . . . left me . . . what'd he leave me for? . . . Mary Collins . . ."

It dawned on me now that Jeremy Waters, Sr., was complaining about Jeremy Waters, Jr.

The Skeleton in the Bed • 137

"Is this your house?" I asked.

"House? There is not a house," the voice came back, somewhat astonished.

"Store place . . . I work here . . . waiting for Jeremy . . . where did they go, Jeremy and Marie . . . his woman . . ."

"How long ago was this?"

"Strange . . . fifty-four . . . where's everyone?"

"Tell me about yourself so I can help you."

"I don't trust you. What have you done with him?"

"What sort of work does he do?"

"A boat. He brings things here."

"When were you born?"

"Twenty-two."

"Where?"

"Hudson village . . ."

"What is your wife's name?"

"Margie."

"Where was she born?"

"Far . . . in Holland."

"Any children?"

"Jeremy . . . three."

When I asked what church he belonged to I got a disdainful snort in reply.

"Churches . . . churches . . . I do not go."

"What sort of place is this?"

"What do you come here for? Fall on your knees . . ." he said, instead, and added, "Find Jeremy . . . he should repent his sins . . . honor thy father and thy mother . . . where am I? There are too many people . . ." The voice sounded confused and worried now.

"And where's his clothes?" he demanded to know.

I started to explain the passage of time.

"Repent, repent," he mumbled, instead, barely listening. "Why did they do it? Hurt me?"

"Who is this woman you mentioned?"

"Maria Goulando." It had sounded like Mary Collins to me at first, but now there was no mistaking the odd name. "She is Jeremy's woman."

"Is he married to her?"

"It is wrong to marry a Catholic," the voice said sternly.

"Is the girl a Catholic?"

"Yes."

"Did he marry her?"

"Over my dead body."

"He didn't marry her then?"

"No . . . the church won."

"Where is the woman now?"

"With Jeremy."

"If you find them, what will you do?"

"Make him repent."

This was said with so much bitterness I decided to take another tack with my questioning. "Have you hurt anyone, Jeremy?" I said.

"Why are you asking me . . . I'm not going to talk," he shot back, defiant again.

"Do you know where you are?"

"Outside the church."

"What church?"

"Lutheran church."

"Are you a Lutheran then?"

"Was . . ."

"What are you now?"

"*Nothing* . . ."

"What street is the church on?"

"Vall Street."

If he meant to say Wall Street he said it with a strange inflection.

I asked him to spell it.

Puzzled and haltingly he said, "Veh—ah—el—el," spelling the W the way a European might spell it, especially a Dutchman or German.

"Wall Street," the voice said more clearly now, this time pronouncing it correctly.

"Name of the church?" I inquired.

"Why—can't—I—find—him?" it came back haltingly.

"What is this place used for?"

"Store things in the back . . ."

"Where do you live?"

"Hudson . . . up the Hudson."

Again I asked for the year he thought we were in.

"Fifty-four . . ."

This is where I made a mistake, perhaps.

"Eighteen fifty-four?" I said. I never like to lead.

"Yes," the voice acknowledged and added, "February . . . today the fifteenth . . ."

"How old are you?" I asked.

"Today is my birthday."

"And your son is not with you?"

"Yes . . . ingratitude shall be his ruin."

"Did you kill anyone?"

"Go away, go away . . ." The voice sounded angry now as if I had hit on a sensitive topic. I reasoned with him, explaining about the passage of time.

"Your son has long died," I explained.

He would not accept this.

"You're a foreigner," he suddenly said, "what do you want? *She's* a foreigner."

"You don't like foreigners?"

"No."

"Did you kill Maria?"

"She was a foreigner," he said with contempt in his voice.

I asked him to make a clean breast of his guilt feelings so that he might free himself from the place we had found him at. There was a long, long pause. Finally he understood and listened quietly as I sent him away to rejoin his dead son. Soon after, I recalled Sybil to her own body. None the worse for her experience, she remembered absolutely nothing that had transpired during the seance.

So there were two ghosts, Jeremy Waters and the girl Maria.

My next step was to check out the names given and see how they connected with the place we were in.

Naturally I assumed that 1854 was the period I should check, since the ghost had acknowledged that date. But there was nothing in the records indicating a Jeremy Waters at that date living on 21st Street.

The only clue of some interest was the name of one James Waters, a "carman" who lived on East 22nd Street between Second and Third Avenues as of 1847, according to Doggett's *New York Directory* for that year. But the thought did not leave me that the "18" was added to the ghost's "54" by my suggestion. Could he have meant 1754?

I decided to check that earlier date. Suddenly things became more interesting.

The entire piece of land on which this and other houses in the block were standing had originally belonged to the Watts family. The Watts city residence stood at 59 East Twenty-first Street and John Watts, Sr., owned the land in 1754, together with his son, John Watts, Jr. I was struck by the similarity of names of father and son, a parallel to Jeremy, Sr., and Jeremy, Jr. They had acquired the land in 1747 from James De Lancey, the elder Watts' brother-in-law. It was then a farm of 130 acres and extended from Twenty-first Street to the East River. Spooner's *Historical Families in America*, which gives these and other details of the prominent Watts family, also states briefly that a third John Watts was born to the young John in 1775, but died unmarried.

I was still struggling with the research on this case, when

Theo Wilson's piece of our seance appeared in the New York *Daily News*. Theo was impressed by the sincerity of both approach and method and reported the investigation factually.

Because of her article a gentleman named Charles Burhaus contacted me with additional information on the Watts family; his father's sister had been married to the last of the Wattses. The Wattses did indeed come from the Hudson Valley and most of them are buried at Tivoli, New York.

The Watts were very religious and fervent Protestants. "Old John" Watts, Mr. Burhaus reports, "disapproved of his son's way of living."

When Mr. Burhaus' grandmother invited his Aunt Minnie to stay at the ancestral Watts house in Tivoli—Mr. Burhaus was then but a child—the lady refused to stay, explaining that the house was haunted by a ghost who liked women.

If there was a storehouse with boats nearby, as the ghost had claimed, on what is now East Twenty-first Street, 1854 would not fit, but 1754 would.

Jeremy Waters and John Watts are not identical names but I have encountered ghost personalities who, for reasons of honor, have disguised their true identities until the skill of the investigator was able to uncover their cover.

So much of the Waters father-and-son relationship seems to fit the Watts father-and-son relationship, the place is correct, and the first names are identical for father and son in both instances, that I cannot help feeling that we have this kind of situation here. If the son ran away with an unacceptable woman, the father would naturally not wish to divulge to a stranger, like me, his true identity, yet he might talk about the events themselves, being emotionally bound to them still.

Miss Nicholson had no further troubles in the apartment after that. She also moved a few weeks later and the new occupants, if they know of my investigation at all, have not seen fit to complain about any disturbances.

So I can only assume that both Jeremy Waters, Sr., and the hapless girl he hurt have found their way across the boundary of the spirit world, which in any event is much nicer than a rooming house on East Twenty-first Street.

One more item gave me food for thought. I had taken a number of still photographs during the two visits to the apartment. When they were developed, several of them showed white shadows and streaks of light that could not be accounted for by natural explanations.

I mailed a set to Dianne Nicholson via first-class mail. It never reached her. A letter, containing some data on the apartment and its past, which she had mailed to me, never reached me about the same time. When I brought the negatives of my pictures to have another set of enlargements made, the lab lost the negatives or rather could not account for them, no reason given.

Finally we had to rephotograph the only existing set of prints to make duplicates.

Coincidence? Perhaps.

If there is such a thing.

11

AN UNUSUAL COMPLAINT

"Good morning," said the wife of the German magazine editor as she put a pot of boiling coffee before him.

"Here's the mail."

Herr Geisler, editor of the German-language magazine *Die Andere Welt,* which means The Other World, quickly glanced through the stack of letters that had to be sorted out.

Ever since he had announced that I would be coming to Germany to look into some *Spukfaelle,* or hauntings, he had been inundated with letters from people who had complaints along those lines. A lot of the letters were the kind you couldn't really sink your teeth into, because the experiences were all personal and individual. And there was a small but weird fringe of disturbed people writing in about psychic experiences that were obviously more psychotic than psychic. Nevertheless, Herr Geisler took his mail call seriously, for the reader is the boss with any good magazine editor.

After he had disposed of the more obvious inquiries he finally turned his attention to the mail inquiring about my coming.

There was one, in particular, that stood out from the rest by the firm, determined handwriting on the envelope.

Without being an expert at graphology, editor Geisler took it for the hand of a young woman or matron. It looked rational and direct and had none of the earmarks of the disturbed individual—people's handwriting often gives away their mental states.

Imagine Herr Geisler's feelings when he opened the letter and read the message. *Ja,* that was something for Hans Holzer all right.

After he reread the letter to make sure he had not imagined its contents, he sent it off to me with the suggestion that I look into the case. The letter, dated May 13, 1966, referred to the announcement of my coming, and then continued:

"For years I have been plagued by a spook. I have recognized the ghost as my husband, wearing a pair of black pants and a white shirt. I should be much obliged to you if you could arrange to have me freed of this spook. I am 84 years old and I like to sleep at night."

Anyone who writes that clearly and precisely at age eighty-four deserved my help, I decided.

I wrote Mrs. Anna S. a brief note informing her of my coming to Hamburg, at which time I would drive out into the suburbs to see and, if possible, to help her.

In July of 1966 my wife and I were in Hamburg, where the local television people had requested an interview. My book *Ghost Hunter* had recently come out in German, and because of this I had consented. But they wanted more: to cover an actual investigation by me.

I had some misgivings about it as I did not know how seriously they would treat the subject, but finally I overcame my suspicions and arranged for the Hamburg TV people to accompany us on the visit to Mrs. S. in a suburb of Hamburg called Lurup. Naturally I had asked the lady if it was all right to film my visit and she had not minded.

We tried very hard to discourage newspapers and just plain curious people, for I wanted to protect the privacy of Mrs. S., but when a big, white TV film truck parks in front of a modern, nondescript apartment building where there is little that is newsworthy, people naturally wonder. We un-packed the gear as quickly as possible—there was a total of five technicians and reporters with us—and then walked up to the apartment occupied by Mrs. S. The old lady mean-while had watched the whole procedure calmly from her window.

Rather than upset her by walking in, all seven people at a time, I used an old method previously tried out with a case in Pittsburgh. First, two people come up and start to chat. Five minutes later, another two ring the bell and are intro-duced, and finally you wonder where are so and so—you need them to be present—and just about then the door bell rings and there they are. By that time the subject has gotten used to the idea of a full house and all proceeds according to plan.

In this case we were met at the door by a smiling, gray-haired woman who belied her years, rapidly moving about and speaking without the slightest hesitation. I detected a strange accent in her voice, foreign to the North German dialect of Hamburg. She later told us she was Hungarian by birth—no wonder the vivacious temperament was not com-patible with the placid North German character!

"What was the first thing you found unusual?" I began the interview. We were seated around a nice, middle-class table covered with a nice, middle-class tablecloth.

"The whole thing started in my kitchen," Mrs. S. began, "at all hours, too. Noises, noises—and nobody there. Then one night I was still lying on my bed—I don't sleep an awful lot—waiting for sleep to come. I looked up, and there is my late husband, wearing his black pants and white shirt."

That, of course, was most upsetting to Mrs. S., inasmuch as her husband had been dead and buried for the past twelve years—since 1944 to be exact.

It appeared that Mr. S. had shared her bed and board for only two years of married bliss. Then a local railroad train brought their idyllic existence to a sudden stop—flagged down, you might say. Mr. S. worked on the railroad, and he had come to the end of his line. Or so Mrs. S. had thought until the racket started up in her kitchen. "Especially my closet," she emphasized. "That's where he stays."

It didn't seem right for a man of the road like Mr. S. to be cooped up in a kitchen closet, but Mrs. S. assured me there was little doubt about it. Regular knocks would announce his presence, and others had heard them too.

Mr. S., however, kept up his visits, always unannounced, always near the closet and looking as he used to look, except for a certain fuzziness around the edges. He never said a word, though, and his widow wondered what on earth—or any place else—he wanted after all this time.

"Do you think there's something disturbing him?" I ventured, in German. But Mrs. S. missed the point.

"Right off the bat he disturbed me, that's what he did," she countered. "Why, my son sat on a chair and he even knocked on that."

But I explained my question again and finally she understood and smiled wryly.

"He was an oddball, he was," she finally said slowly. "Toward the end, well, we had a good marriage, but the last six months of our life together we didn't live together."

Aha! I thought. Remorse!

Evidently the red-hot grandmamma didn't get all she expected from Mr. S. and it troubled him still. Nothing like a good man letting an even better woman down.

Nothing, however, indicated any unfinished business on his part. Mrs. S. lived on a decent pension and at least in that respect Mr. S. had taken good care of his wife.

"I've had lots of holy masses said for him," Mrs. S. explained. "I've told him not to worry about anything any longer, but he keeps bothering me."

"Why do you suppose he does this?"

"I think he was sorry he married me. After he came back from his brother's funeral, he started to act kind of funny. It had to do with his sister-in-law. I think he would have married her if we had not been married already."

Because she was afraid of the visitations of her late husband—and, incidentally, his attentions—she took in a boarder, a young man. She felt better with a man around the house, she explained.

"Attentions?" I asked.

"Yes," she nodded gravely and somewhat with embarrassment. "I felt him next to me in bed. I know it was him. I recognized his touch."

I explained that it looked to me as though her late husband had settled for her after all, and not the sister-in-law. Perhaps if she accepted his posthumous favors in the spirit in which they were given?

I instructed her how to deal with Mr. S. next time he showed himself.

To tell him, "I love you, yes, but please go away and don't bother me. And about those six months when you weren't much good—forget it, it was nice to have a rest. Above all, don't feel guilty."

She understood what the problem was now.

Was there any problem between them because of their different religions? She was Catholic and he was Protestant, and the holy masses had been Catholic masses.

"Oh, no," she replied, "it wouldn't have mattered to him. He didn't believe in anything."

There was a rustling in back of us. I had become so engrossed in my interview with the spunky eighty-four-year-old lady that I had completely forgotten about *Das Hamburg Fernsehen*, the Hamburg TV people, who had been filming the scene furiously There remained only the actual exorcism ceremony to be done. I waited until the cameraman had changed magazines, then I instructed Mrs. S. to repeat after me, word for word, sentence for sentence.

"Adolph Paul S.," I began, "you are not to come here any longer."

"Any longer," Mrs. S. repeated.

"I have forgiven you, I love you, but the time has come for you to join your relatives."

"Join your relatives," intoned Mrs. S. I discovered an urgency I had not put into my own words. Perhaps the thought of sending him home to his relatives was particularly pleasing to her.

"Go in peace, and don't return here any more. The door is closed."

"Closed," repeated Mrs. S. and looked up at me.

The television people started to pack their gear. Mrs. S. broke out some *Schnaps,* insisting we join her in a glass of the good stuff, to celebrate the expected departure of her late husband to territories whence no train returns.

I smiled at her. She was full of life and her eyes sparkled. Eighty-four, I thought, my God, she's going to be around another fifty years.

"Even my boarder heard it," she suddenly said. We had forgotten about the boarder.

"What about him?" I questioned her.

Klaus W., a young man who worked in the market, had not only told her about his troubles with the ghost—he had also told his mother. Mother had come and talked about it with Mrs. S.

"Three times it happened," Mrs. S. said, "and each time I told him it was just the passing cars. After all, I didn't want to lose him."

But there were those strange, knocking noises in the middle of the night.

In the end, Klaus couldn't take it any more. He moved out, but recommended a friend for the vacant room.

Either the husband doesn't like to talk to the new boarder or the new boarder sleeps more soundly than his predecessor, but so far there had been no complaints.

Mrs. S. then insisted we should look at her kitchen cabinet where she had heard all the noises and where her husband had been "in residence."

"That's how he did it," she said sharply and rapped on the wood, "knocking, knocking, knocking!"

She was getting excited again and I reminded her that we had, after all, sent Mr. S. to his just rewards.

I shook hands with Mrs. S., and we left. The television people weren't sure when the station would run the film. Fortunately they ran it after our departure from Hamburg. Had they shown it during my stay, there would have been considerable damage among TV executives. A friend of mine saw the resulting film. It was all very factual except for a small epilogue by a station spokesman questioning my honesty. The next time a Hamburg TV man wants an interview I will refer him to the nearest practitioner of black magic. For a treatment.

Two weeks later I had a letter from Mrs. S. It would seem that the press was bothering her since the TV film had been shown. In fact, it was worse than being bothered by her late husband. And speaking of the devil—that is, actually, her late husband—things weren't going well at all.

The knocking continued and the prickling sensation she had so often felt when the dear departed one was hovering around, was back again. Could I please come back and do it all over again? And bring a medium?

I felt genuinely sorry for the old lady and I explained what I had not had the courage to say before. That it was her continuing demands on an active life, and her unusual overabundance of that same life force, that kept supplying the energy for the phenomena.

Could she sublimate these desires and "retire" from her

active memories into a more peaceful old age? After all, she was eighty-four years old and it would be best if she directed her thoughts toward less exciting subjects than husbands, late or living.

But you know how those Hungarians are.

12

WESTWARD HO ON THE SPECTRAL TRAIL

Little did I know when I had successfully investigated the haunted apartment of Mrs. Verna Kunze in San Bernardino, that Mrs. Kunze would lead me to another case equally as interesting as her own, which I have reported on in my recent book, *Ghosts of the Golden West*.

Mrs. Kunze is a very well-organized person and a former employee in the passport division of the State Department. She is used to sifting facts from fancy. Her interest in psycho-cybernetics had led her to a group of like-minded individuals meeting regularly in Orange County. There she met a gentleman formerly with the FBI, by the name of Walter Tipton.

One day Mr. Tipton asked her help in contacting me concerning a most unusual case that had been brought to his attention. Having checked out some of the more obvious details, he had found the people involved truthful and worthy of my time.

So it was that I heard for the first time of Mrs. Carole Trausch of Santa Ana at the end of January 1967.

What has happened to the Trausch family and their neighbors is not just a ghost story. Far more than that they found themselves in the middle of an old tragedy that had not yet been played out fully when they moved into their spanking new home.

Carole Trausch was born in Los Angeles of Scottish parentage and went to school in Los Angeles. Her father is a retired policeman and her mother Scotland-born. She married quite young and moved with her husband, a businessman, to live first in Huntington Beach and later in Westminster, near Santa Ana.

Now in her early twenties, she is a glamorous-looking blonde who belies the fact that she has three children aged eight, six, and two, all girls.

Early in 1966 they moved into one of two hundred two-story bungalows in a new development in Westminster. They were just an ordinary family without any particular interest in the occult. About their only link with the world of the psychic were some peculiar dreams Carole had had.

The first time was when she was still a little girl. She dreamed there were some pennies hidden in their rose bed in the garden. On awakening, she laughed at herself, but out of curiosity she did go to the rose bed and looked. Sure enough, there were some pennies in the soil below the roses. Many times since then she has dreamed of future events which later came true.

One night she dreamed that her husband's father was being rolled on a stretcher down a hospital corridor by a nurse on his way to an operation. The next morning there was a phone call informing them that such an emergency had indeed taken place about the time she dreamed it. On several occasions she sensed impending accidents or other unpleasantnesses. But she is not always sure what kind. One day she felt sure she or her husband would be in a car accident. Instead, it was one of her little girls, who was hit by a passing car.

When they moved into their present house, Mrs. Trausch took an immediate dislike to it. This upset her practically-minded husband. They had hardly been installed when she begged him to move again. He refused.

The house is a white-painted two-story bungalow, which was built about five years before their arrival. Downstairs is a large, oblong living room, a kitchen, and a dining area. On the right, the staircase leads to the upper story. The landing is covered with linoleum, and there are two square bedrooms, on each side of the landing, with wall-to-wall carpeting and windows giving onto the yard in the case of the rear bedroom and onto the street in the front room.

There is a large closet along the south wall of the rear bedroom. Nothing about the house is unusual and there was neither legend nor story nor rumor attached to the house when they rented it from the owners, a local bank.

And yet there was something queer about the house. Mrs. Trausch's nerves were on edge right from the very first when they moved in. But she accepted her husband's decision to stay put and swept her own fears under the carpet of every-day reason, as the first weeks in their new home rolled by.

At first the children would come to her with strange tales. The six-year-old girl would complain of being touched by someone she could not see whenever she dropped off for her afternoon nap in the bedroom upstairs. Sometimes this presence would shake the bed and then there was a shrill noise, somewhat like a beep, coming from the clothes closet. The oldest girl, eight years old, confirmed the story and reported similar experiences in the room.

Carole dismissed these reports as typical imaginary tales of the kind children will tell.

But one day she was resting on the same bed upstairs and found herself being tapped on the leg by some unseen person.

This was not her imagination, she was fully awake, and it

made her wonder if perhaps her intuition about this house had not been right all along.

She kept experiencing the sensation of touch in the upstairs bedrooms only, and it got to be a habit with her to make the beds as quickly as possible and then rush downstairs where she felt nothing unusual. Then she also began to hear the shrill, beeplike sounds coming from the closet. She took out all the children's clothes and found nothing that could have caused the noise. Finally she told her husband about it and he promptly checked the pipes and other structural details of the house, only to shake his head. Nothing could have made such noises.

For several months she had kept her secret, but now that her husband also knew, she had Diane, the oldest, tell Daddy about it as well.

It was about this time that she became increasingly aware of a continuing presence upstairs. Several times she would hear footsteps walking upstairs, and on investigation found the children fast asleep. Soon the shuffling steps would be regular features of the house. It would always start near the closet in the rear bedroom, and go toward the stair landing.

Carole began to wonder if her nerves weren't getting the better of her, so she was much relieved one day when her sister, Kathleen Bachelor, who had come to visit her, remarked about the strange footsteps upstairs. Both women knew the children were out. Only the baby was upstairs, and on rushing up the stairs they found her safely asleep in her crib. It had sounded to them like a small person wearing slippers.

Soon she discovered, however, that there were two kinds of footsteps: the furtive pitter-patter of a child and the heavy, deliberate footfalls of a grownup.

Had they fallen heir to two ghosts? The thought seemed farfetched even to ESP-prone Carole, but it could not be dismissed entirely. What was going on, she wondered. Evidently she was not losing her mind, for others had also heard these things.

Once she had gone out for the evening and when she returned around 10:30 P.M., she dismissed the babysitter. After the girl had left, she was alone with the baby. Suddenly she heard the water running in the bathroom upstairs. She raced up the stairs and found the bathroom door shut tight. Opening it, she noticed that the water was on, and there was some water in the sink.

On January 27, 1967, Carole had guests for lunch, two neighbors named Pauline J. and Joyce S., both young women about the same age as Carole. Now the children all sleep in the same upstairs front bedroom, the two older girls sharing the bed while the baby girl occupies the crib. The baby had her nap between 11:30 and 2 P.M. At noon, however, the baby woke up crying, and, being barely able to talk at age two, kept saying "Baby scared, Mommy!"

The three ladies had earlier been upstairs together, preparing the baby for her crib. At that time they had also put the entire room carefully in order, paying particular attention to making the covers and spread on the large bed very smooth and setting up the dolls and toys on the chest in the corner.

When the baby cried at noon, all three women went upstairs and found the bed had wrinkles and an imprint as though someone had been sitting on it. The baby, of course, was still in her crib.

They picked up the child and went downstairs with her. Just as they got to the stairway, all three heard an invisible child falling down the stairs about three steps ahead of where they were standing.

It was after this experience that Mrs. Trausch wondered why the ghost child never touched any of the dolls. You see, the footsteps they kept hearing overhead always went from the closet to the toy chest where the dolls are kept. But none of the dolls was ever disturbed. It occurred to her that the invisible child was a boy, and there were no boy's toys around.

The sounds of a child running around in the room upstairs became more and more frequent; she knew it was not one of her children, having accounted for her own in other ways. The whole situation began to press on her nerves and even her husband—who had until now tended to shrug off what he could not understand—became concerned. Feelers were put out to have me come to the house as soon as possible, but I could not make it right away and they would have to cope with their unseen visitors for the time being, or until I arrived on the scene.

All during February the phenomena continued, so much so that Mrs. Trausch began to take them as part of her routine. But she kept as much to the downstairs portion of the house as she could. For some unknown reason the phenomena never intruded on that part of the house.

She called in the lady who managed the development for the owners and cautiously told her of their problem. But the manager knew nothing whatever about the place except that it was new and to her knowledge no great tragedies had occurred there in her own time.

When the pitter-patter of the little feet continued, Carole Trausch decided she just had to know. On March 16, 1967, she decided to place some white flour on the linoleum-covered portion of the upstairs floor to trap the unseen child. This was the spot where the footsteps were most often heard and for the past two days the ghost child had indeed "come out" there to run and play.

In addition she took a glass of water with some measuring spoons of graduated sizes in it, setting it all down in a small pan and put it into her baby's crib, with a cracker in the pan beside the glass. This was the sort of thing a little child might want—that is, a child in the world of flesh and blood.

She then retired to the downstairs portion of the house and called in a neighbor. Together the two women kept watch, waiting for the early afternoon hours when the ghost child usually became active upstairs.

As the minutes ticked off, Carole began to wonder how she would look if nothing happened. The neighbor probably would consider her neurotic, and accuse her of making up the whole story as an attention-getter in this rather quiet community.

But she did not have to worry long. Sure enough, there were the footsteps again upstairs. The two women waited a few moments to give the ghost a chance to leave an impression, then they rushed upstairs.

They saw no child, but the white flour had indeed been touched. There were footmarks in the flour, little feet that seemed unusually small and slender. Next to the prints there was the picture of a flower as if the child had bent down and finger-painted the flower as a sign of continuing presence. From the footprints, they took the child to be between three and four years of age. The water and pan in the crib had not been touched and as they stood next to the footprints, there was utter silence around them.

Mrs. Trausch now addressed the unseen child gently and softly and promised the child they would not hurt it. Then she placed some boy's toys which she had obtained for this occasion around the children's room and withdrew.

There was no immediate reaction to all this. But two days later, the eight-year-old daughter came running down the stairs to report she had seen the shadow of a little boy in front of the linen closet in the hall. He wore a striped shirt and pants and was shorter than she was.

When I heard of the footprints by telephone, I set the week of June 2 for a visit to the house. Meanwhile I instructed the Trausches to continue observing what they could.

But the Trausches had already resolved to leave the house even if I should be able to resolve their "problem." No matter what, they could never be quite sure. And living with a ghost—or perhaps two ghosts—was not what they wanted to do, what with three lively children to keep them on their toes.

Across from the Trausch apartment and separated from it by a narrow lane is another house, just like it and built about the same time on what was before only open farmland—as far as everyone there knows. In 1963 the area was flooded and was condemned, but it dried out later. There is and always has been plenty of water in the area, a lowland studded with ponds and fishing holes.

The neighbor's name was Bonnie Swanson and she too was plagued by footsteps that had no human agency causing them. The curious thing is that these phenomena were heard only in the upstairs portion of their house, where the bedrooms are, just as with the Trausch house.

Twice the Swansons called in police, only to be told that there was no one about causing the footsteps. In April the Swansons had gone away for a weekend, taking their child with them. When they returned, the husband opened the door and was first to step into the house. At this moment he distinctly heard footsteps running very fast from front to rear of the rooms, as if someone had been surprised by their return. Mrs. Swanson, who had also heard this, joined her husband in looking over the house, but there was no stranger about, and no one could have left.

Suddenly they became aware of the fact that a light upstairs was burning. They knew they had turned it off when they left. Moreover, in the kitchen they almost fell over a child's tricycle. Last time they saw this tricycle it stood in the corner of their living room. It could not have gotten to the kitchen by itself and there was no sign of anyone breaking and entering in their absence. Nothing was missing.

It seemed as if my approaching visit was somehow getting through to the ghost or ghosts, for as the month of June came closer, the phenomena seemed to mount in intensity and frequency.

On the morning of May 10, 1967, at nine-thirty, Mrs. Trausch was at her front bedroom window, opening the window to let in the air. From her window she could see directly into the Swenson house, since both houses were on the same level and the windows parallel to each other. As she reached her window and casually looked out across to the Swenson's rooms, which she knew to be empty at this time of day—Mr. Swenson at work, and Mrs. Swenson and a house guest out for the morning—she saw to her horror the arm of a woman pushing back the curtain of Mrs. Swenson's window.

There was a curiously stiff quality about this arm and the way it moved the curtain back. And then she saw clearly a woman with a deathlike white mask of a face staring at her. The woman's eyes were particularly odd. Despite her excitement, Mrs. Trausch noticed that the woman had wet hair and was dressed in something filmy, like a white nylon negligee, which had pink flowers on it.

For the moment, Mrs. Trausch assumed that the house guest must somehow have stayed behind, and so she smiled at the woman across from her. Then the curtain dropped and the woman disappeared. Carole Trausch could barely wait to question her neighbor about the incident. There hadn't been anyone at the house when she saw the woman with the wet hair.

Now Mrs. Trausch was sure that there were two of them, two unseen visitors, a child and a woman, which would account for the different quality of the footsteps they had been hearing.

She decided to try and find out more about the land on which the house stood. A neighbor living a few blocks away on Chestnut Street, who had been in her house for over twenty years, managed to supply some additional information. Long before the development had been built, there had been a farm there.

In the exact place where the Trausches now lived, there had been a barn. When the house was built, a large trench was dug and the barn pushed into it and burned. The people who lived there at the time were a Mexican family named Felix. They had a house nearby but sold the area of the farm to the builders.

But because of the flooded condition of the area, the houses stood vacant for a few years. Only after extensive drainage had taken place did the houses become inhabitable and the Trausches were able to move into theirs. The area was predominantly Mexican and the development a kind of Anglo-Saxon island in their midst.

All this information was brought out only after our visit, incidentally, and neither Sybil Leek, who acted as my medium, nor I had any knowledge of it at the time.

Mrs. Trausch was not the only adult member of the family to witness the phenomena. Her husband finally confessed that on several occasions he had been puzzled by footsteps upstairs when he came home late at night. That was around 1 A.M., and when he checked to see if any of the children had gotten out of bed, he found them fast asleep. Mr. Trausch is a very realistic man. His business is manufacturing industrial tools. He does not believe in ghosts. But he heard the footsteps too.

The Trausches also realized that the shuffling footsteps of what appeared to be a small child always started up as soon as the two older girls had left for school. It was as if the invisible boy wanted to play with their toys when they weren't watching.

Also, the ghost evidently liked the bathroom and water, for the steps resounded most often in that area. On one occasion Mrs. Trausch was actually using the bathroom when the steps resounded next to her. Needless to say, she left the bathroom in a hurry.

Finally the big day had arrived. Mr. Trausch drove his Volkswagen all the way to Hollywood to pick up Mrs. Leek and myself, and while he did not believe in ghosts, he didn't scoff at them either.

After a pleasant ride of about two hours, we arrived at Westminster. It was a hot day in June, as the Santa Ana area is known for its warm climate. Mr. Trausch parked the car and we went into the house where the rest of the family was already awaiting our visit.

I asked Sybil to scout around for any clairvoyant impressions she might get of the situation and as she did so I followed her around the house with my faithful tape recorder so that not a word might be lost.

As soon as Sybil had set foot in the house, she pointed to the staircase and intoned ominously, "It's upstairs."

Then, with me trailing, she walked up the stairs as gingerly as a trapeze artist while I puffed after her.

"Gooseflesh," she announced and held out her arm. Now whenever we are in a haunted area Sybil does get gooseflesh —not because she is scared but because it is a natural instant reaction to whatever presence might be there.

We were in the parents' room now and Sybil looked around with the expectant smile of a well-trained bird dog casing the moors.

"Two conflicting types," she then announced. "There's anger and resentfulness toward someone. There's something here. Has to do with the land. Two people."

She explained she felt it centered in the children's room, and that there was a vicious element surrounding it, an element of destruction. We walked into the children's room and immediately she made for the big closet in the rear. Behind that wall there was another apartment, but the Trausches did not know anything about it except that the people in it had recently just moved in.

"It's that side," Sybil announced and waved toward the backyard of the house where numerous children of various ages were playing with the customary racket accompanying it.

"Vincent," Sybil added, out of the blue. "Maybe I don't have the accent right, but it is Vincent. But it is connected with all this. Incidentally, it is the land that's causing the trouble, not the house itself."

The area which Sybil had pointed out just a moment before as being the center of the activities was the exact spot where the old barn had once stood.

"It's nothing against this house," Sybil said to Mrs. Trausch, "but something out of the past. I'd say 1925. The name Vincent is important. There's fire involved. I don't feel a person here but an influence . . . a thing. This is different from our usual work. It's the upper part of the building where the evil was."

I then eased Sybil into a chair in the children's room and we grouped ourselves silently around her, waiting for some form of manifestation to take place.

Mrs. Trausch was nervously biting her lips but otherwise bearing up under what must have been the culmination of a long and great strain for her. Sybil was relaxing now, but she was still awake.

"There's some connection with a child," she said now, "a lost child . . . 1925 . . . the child was found here, dead."

"Whose child is it?" I pressed.

"Connected with Vincent . . . dark child . . . nine years old . . . a boy . . . the children here have to be careful . . ."

"Does this child have any connection with the house?"

"He is lost."

"Can you see him; can he see you?"

"I see him. Corner . . . the barn. He broke his neck. Two

men . . . hit the child, they didn't like children, you see . . . they left him . . . until he was found . . . woman . . . Fairley . . . name . . . Pete Fairley . . ."

By now Sybil had glided into a semi-trance and I kept up the barrage of questions to reconstruct the drama in the barn.

"Do they live here?" I inquired.

"Nobody lives here. Woman walked from the water to find the boy. He's dead. She has connection with the two men who killed him. Maniacs, against children."

"What is her connection with the boy?"

"She had him, then she lost him. She looked after him."

"Who were the boy's parents then?"

"Fairley. Peter Fairley. 1925."

Sybil sounded almost like a robot now, giving the requested information.

"What happened to the woman?" I wanted to know.

"Mad . . . she found the boy dead, went to the men . . . there was a fight . . . she fell in the water . . . men are here . . . there's a fire . . ."

"Who were these men?"

"Vincent . . . brothers . . . nobody is very healthy in this farm . . . don't like women . . ."

"Where did the child come from?"

"Lost . . . from the riverside . . ."

"Can you see the woman?"

"A little . . . the boy I can see clearly."

It occurred to me how remarkable it was for Sybil to speak of a woman who had fallen into the water when the apparition Mrs. Trausch had seen had had wet hair. No one had discussed anything about the house in front of Sybil, of course. So she had no way of knowing that the area had once been a farm, or that a barn had stood there where she felt the disturbances centered. Nor that it was a child the people in the house kept hearing upstairs.

"The woman is out of tempo," Sybil explained. "That makes it difficult to see her. The boy is frightened."

Sybil turned her attention to the little one now and, with my prodding, started to send him away from there.

"Peter go out and play with the children . . . outside," she pleaded.

"And his parents . . . they are looking for him." I added.

"He wants the children here to go with him," Sybil came back.

Mrs. Trausch started to swallow nervously.

"Tell him he is to go first," I instructed.

"He wants to have the fair woman come with him," Sybil explained and I suggested that the two of them go.

"She understands," Sybil explained, "and is willing, but he is difficult. He wants the children."

I kept pleading with the ghost boy. Nothing is harder than dealing with a lost one so young.

"Join the other children. They are already outside," I said.

There was a moment of silence, interrupted only by the muffled sounds of living children playing outside.

"Are they still here?" I cautiously inquired a little later.

"Can't see them now, but I can see the building. Two floors. Nobody there now."

I decided it was time to break the trance which had gradually deepened and at this point was a full trance. A moment later Sybil Leek "was back."

Now we discussed the matter freely and I researched the information just obtained.

As I understood it, there had been this boy, age nine, Peter Fairley by name, who had somehow gotten away from his nanny, a fair woman. He had run into a farm and gone up to the upper story of a barn where two brothers named Vincent had killed him. When the woman found him, she went mad. Then she looked for the men whom she knew and there was a fight during which she was drowned. The two of them are ghosts because they are lost; the boy lost in a strange place and the woman lost in guilt for having lost the boy.

Mrs. Kunze and Mrs. Trausch volunteered to go through the local register to check out the names and to see if anything bearing on this tragedy could be found in print.

Unfortunately the death records for the year 1925 were incomplete, Mrs. Trausch discovered at the Santa Ana *Register*, and even at the local Hall of Records in the Court House. The County Sheriff's Office was of no help, either. But they found an interesting item in the *Register* of January 1, 1925:

> Deputies probe tale of "burial" in orange grove. Several Deputy Sheriffs, in a hurried call to Stanton late last night, failed to find any trace of several men who were reported to be "burying something" in an isolated orange grove near that town, as reported to them at the Sheriff's office here.
>
> Officers rushing to the scene were working under the impression that a murder had been committed and that the body was being interred, but a thorough search in that vicinity failed to reveal anything unusual, according to a report made by Chief Criminal Deputy Ed Mc-Clellan, on their return. Deputy Sheriffs Joe Scott and Joe Ryan accompanied McClellan.

Mrs. Kunze, a long-time resident of the area and quite familiar with its peculiarities, commented that such a burial in an isolated orange grove could easily have been covered up by men familiar with the irrigating system, by flooding that section, thus erasing all evidence of a newly made grave.

I wondered about the name Peter Fairley. Of course I did not expect to find the boy listed somewhere, but was there a Fairley family in these parts in 1925?

There was.

In the Santa Ana County Directories, S.W. Section, for the year 1925, there is a listing for a Frank Fairley, carpenter, at 930 W. Bishop, Santa Ana. The listing continues at the same address the following year also. It was not in the 1924 edition of the directory, however, so perhaps the Fairleys were new to the area then.

At the outset of the visit Mrs. Leek had mentioned a Felix connected with the area. Again consulting the County Directories for 1925, we found several members of the Felix family listed. Andres Felix, rancher, at Golden West Avenue and Bolsa Chica Road, post office Westminster, Adolph and Miguel Felix, laborers, at the same address—perhaps brothers—and Florentino Felix, also a rancher, at a short distance from the farm of Andres Felix. The listing also appears in 1926.

No Vincent or Vincente, however. But of course not all members of the family need to have been listed. The directories generally list only principals, i.e., those gainfully employed or owners of business or property. Then again, there may have been two hired hands by that name, if Vincente was a given name rather than a Christian name.

The 1911 *History of Orange County* by Samuel Armor described the area as consisting of a store, church, school, and a few residences only. It was then called Bolsa, and the main area was used as ranch and stock land. The area abounds in fish hatcheries also, which were started around 1921 by a Japanese named Akiyama. Thus the existence of water holes in the area and of fish tanks, as well as natural lakes.

With the help of Mrs. Kunze I came across still another interesting record.

According to the Los Angeles *Times* of January 22, 1956, "an ancient residence at 14611 Golden West Street, Westminster, built 85 years ago, was razed for subdivision." This was undoubtedly the farm residence and land on which the development we had been investigating was later built.

And there we have the evidence. Three names are given by our psychic friend: Felix, Vincent, and Peter Fairley. Two of them are found in the printed record, with some difficulty, and with the help of local researchers familiar with the source material, which neither Mrs. Leek nor I was prior to the visit to the haunted house. The body of the woman could easily have been disposed of without leaving a trace by dumping it into one of the fish tanks or other water holes in the area, or perhaps in the nearby Santa Ana River.

About a month after our investigation, the Trausch family moved back to Huntington Beach, leaving the Westminster house to someone else, who might some day appear on the scene.

But Carole Trausch informed me that from the moment of our investigation onward not a single incident had marred the peace of their house.

So I can only assume that Sybil and I were able to help the two unfortunate ghosts out into the open, the boy to find his parents, no doubt also on his side of the veil, and the woman to find peace and forgiveness for her negligence. in allowing the boy to be killed.

It is not always possible for the Psychic Investigator to leave a haunted house free of its unseen inhabitants, and when it does happen, then the success is its own reward.

13

ARE THERE SUCH THINGS AS "LIVING" GHOSTS?

As my investigations of psychic phenomena mounted in number and importance, it became increasingly clear to me that ghosts and spirits and human beings must all have something in common: if a living person can turn into a "dead" spirit or ghost, then that which survives must already have been contained within mortal man. We are as much spirit in our lifetime as we'll ever be.

I also noticed an amazing analogy between certain sleep and dream states and death—as reported by those claiming to be surviving entities speaking through entranced mediums.

The seat of personality seems encased within a temporary frame called the physical body. Under certain conditions, the personality (or soul, if you want to be religious-minded) can emerge from the "box" and behave independently of it. This is called astral travel, or out-of-the-body experience. Here the separation is temporary and still under the control of the traveler—the sleeper. At death the separation is permanent and the personality, the inner self, leaves the "box" behind, rising to a new and freer existence in what Dr. Joseph Rhine of Duke University has called the world of the mind and what I prefer calling the non-physical world.

But there are cases where a ghost appears and on checking it is found that the one whose ghost it is is still alive and kicking.

Are there such things as "living ghosts"?

In 1920 Mrs. L. lived in a small oil town in Oklahoma. Her husband was a drilling contractor and their lives were ordinary lives without a trace of the uncanny. One morning Mrs. L. awoke to the sound of a buzzer that preceded the sounding of the hour on her alarm clock. She opened her eyes and noticed it was 7 A.M., or rather five minutes before the hour. In direct line between her eyes and the wall was a chest of drawers. Between the chest and the window there was some space, and as her eyes fastened themselves on that area, she became aware of a figure standing there. It was her husband, staring straight at her. However, she noticed that the apparition ended at the knees where the figure faded out. He wore his usual tan pants, but she also noticed a white shirt with purple stripes. What puzzled her about this shirt was the fact that it was at this moment neatly tucked away inside the chest of drawers.

Now the figure of her husband started to fade away, slowly, from the bottom on up. By the time the apparition had fully dissolved, the clock chimed the hour—seven o'clock.

Mrs. L. got up quickly and opened the chest of drawers; there was the shirt. Before she realized what she was doing, she had torn the shirt to bits!

A short time after, Mr. L. was involved in an explosion at the oil rig where he worked. He was blown into a wheelhouse and knocked unconscious. Everything around him was on fire, but he came to just in time to grab a plank and kick it out of the wheelhouse, and thus make his escape.

At the time she saw her husband's "ghost," Mrs. L. was

sure he was alive. She was equally convinced that it was a kind of warning. If she hadn't destroyed the telltale shirt and if he had worn it that fatal day, would he have been able to save himself?

A tantalizing question.

"Haven't seen a ghost now for about two years," confided the lady from New Britain, Connecticut, who had come to hear my lecture at the college.

It turned out she had seen ghosts galore before that date, however. Mrs. Lillian Dorval had a husband, a daughter, and a lot of common sense. But she is very psychic, like it or not.

The first time anything unusual happened was in 1957. She had just fed the baby her bottle and fallen asleep, around midnight. Suddenly she awoke to see what she thought was her husband standing beside her bed. It was 2 A.M. When she asked him what he was doing, standing there like that, he did not answer. So Mrs. Dorval reached over and switched on the light. There in bed beside her was her husband, sleeping peacefully.

When she explained that she had just seen him standing near her bed, he thought she had had a nightmare. But she had no doubt about it—she knew she had been awake. What she did not know at the time was that she had just undergone an experience of bi-location. Mrs. Dorval encountered the "living ghosts" again, some time after her husband had passed away unexpectedly. A friend of hers had left her and she had gone to bed. In the middle of the night she saw his apparition standing by her bed. He was very much alive at the moment she saw him, perhaps still thinking of their evening together.

In November 1966 she saw an apparition of a man she could not recognize at the time. Again it was in the very heart of the night, around 1 A.M.

Several months later she met this man and became friendly

with him. Obviously he had been alive at the time she saw his apparition—but how could one explain this link, since she had not yet encountered him, nor he her, except by prevision on her part.

"Regular" ghosts—that is, of dead people—are nothing new to her, of course.

Take her favorite uncle, Harry, for instance. Five days after the family had buried him, there he stood on the right side of her bed. All the "living ghosts," projections of people still in the body, had always appeared on her *left* side. Moreover, the living ones were in color while Uncle Harry wore a plain white suit. When she switched the lights on, he melted away like the others.

Mrs. Dorval fears ridicule so she has not seen fit to talk about her experiences. She also has had out-of-the-body experiences of her own when she found herself soaring out onto rooftops and trees. And the incident she remembers most vividly was her neighbor's funeral which she attended. While the proceedings went forward in the customary manner, she noticed the neighbor sitting on a wall near the casket, laughing and looking over the mourners.

Projections of living people, or "Phantasms of the Living," as the author Sidgwick has called them, occur when a person's thoughts are so strongly engaged at a distance that part of their personality travels with them. If the person on the other end of the "line" happens to be receptive, that is, a psychic person "in tune" with the sender, reception of an image or even a voice may result. And yet, by nature, the ghosts of the living and the ghosts of the dead have much in common. Both prove by the sheer weight of the evidence—numerous as these cases are—that man possesses an indestructible inner self which is capable of breaking through the conventional limits of time and space.

But apparitions of the living and ghosts of the dead have a common frontier in the type of ghost that refuses to accept the facts of afterlife. These people are aware that they are not what they used to be but persist in their habits in what was formerly their world. In a way, they too are psychotic in the sense every ghost is disturbed, but their aberration is more refined, more sophisticated than that of the "run of the mill" specter unable to recognize its own demise.

A young lady by the name of Shaaron Kennett, in an eastern New England city, has lived with her psychic experiences without too much concern. So what if several relatives have dropped in on her at the precise moment of their deaths? Distance has no bearing on these visitations. Miss Kennett was in Rhode Island once and the dead left this world in Philadelphia, but the twain met in Miss Kennett's bedroom at the very instance of death.

In 1962 the young lady moved into an old house in town, along with her parents and a brother. Two weeks after they had installed themselves Miss Kennett was startled to find another person in the house, a person who could not be accounted for as a visitor or otherwise. The woman was clearly visible in the downstairs bedroom, so clearly, in fact, that Miss Kennett had a good chance to look at her carefully. Her stern face was what struck her strongly, and she wore a plain, dark dress with high neck and a thin strip of lace at the throat. Her steel-gray hair was pulled back severely from her face. The woman was of medium height, very slight build, and seemed elderly.

After this initial experience when Miss Kennett saw the woman for several seconds before she disappeared, the ghostly occupant of the house returned a number of times. Soon she would show up all over the house, day or night, meeting the family at the top of the stairs and always looking them over before "allowing" them to pass, then descending the stairs herself. Miss Kennett's mother also saw her, so much so that it became a daily routine for her to see the ghost woman in her kitchen first thing every morning.

The stern expression on her face never changed and though the family accepted their "house ghost," the dogs and cats did not and kept out of her way.

Miss Kennett made some discreet inquiries about their house. She was able to trace the apparition to a former owner of their house, a Mrs. Frances F. The lady evidently felt the house was still hers, and the downstairs bedroom in which she first appeared to Shaaron Kennett was indeed her former bedroom. What were strangers doing in *her* house? What sort of people are going up *her* staircase? Look at it from the ghost's point of view, if you please.

I daresay that at least one per cent of all those who die either unhappily or with some unfinished business on their minds may stay behind in what was for so long their proper home.

Ghosts are always the personalities of people who died tragically, it is true, but this death need not be sudden.

Lingering suffering, mental or physical, can result in the same type of phenomenon.

My files are bulging with such cases, verified properly and containing the eyewitness—or sometimes ear witness—reports of reputable people.

Neither are the ones clinging to their former abodes spirits in the sense that all of us turn spirit at death, if death occurs normally and is accepted by us as such.

The natural order of things is to leave one's physical surroundings at the time the physical body is left behind.

Those refusing to leave are therefore in violation of this rule and become like fish out of water: of spirit "matter," yet within the physical world, they are part of neither one.

The stay-behinds are a real problem only when they become so filled with hatred for those succeeding them in their former homes that they attempt to drive them out, by whatever means are at their command.

Thus the *Poltergeist* or physical phenomena stage is

reached, when frightening movements of objects, noises and other manifestations occur and convince the living that theirs is not a safe place to be. Unfortunately people are filled with fears of the Unknown. They often do give in and move out, leaving the stay-behind dead in command. In so doing, they condemn the stay-behinds to a far worse existence than being dead—an in-between state where no progress is possible.

Until people became used to my ideas of contacting the stay-behinds through trance mediums, there was really little they could do: either stay and endure the shenanigans, or leave and let the stay-behinds have the house, or perhaps rent it to some other tenant with thicker skin.

Not everybody is psychic in the same degree. The majority of people are so insensitive they may not even notice a stay-behind. But a substantial minority do get impressions of them ranging all the way from a mere "uneasy feeling of a presence" to full sight of the dead one. This is why not everybody experiences the presences by merely walking into a place plagued by stay-behinds. One cannot request a command performance by the stay-behind just so one can prove that he or she is always there. They are, having no other place to go to.

Often enough, they frequent a certain room or even a favorite piece of furniture.

Having imparted much of their personal aura or magnetism to the object through long years of bodily contact with it, they naturally are drawn to it both by sentimental memory and by automatic attraction. If a stranger sits in their favorite chair, quite rightly the stay-behind will deeply resent the intrusion. To the stay-behind the living are the intruders in *his* world, not the other way round. He neither comprehends nor cares to know that things have changed through his death.

It is futile to walk into an old house in the hope of encountering a "ghost," just because the house has been lived in for a long time and perhaps has seen many and varied emotional scenes, or even violent death or struggle.

What the sensitive person might feel in such a place would be an impression of past events rather than participants in them.

On the other hand, some such houses do have ghosts or stay-behinds in them. But then one should rather expect someone among the living, sooner or later, to have an experience of an objective kind, an experience of either seeing or hearing the stay-behind. I, for one, would never investigate a house unless and until several reputable people reported to me that they had indeed had an unusual firsthand experience in the house in question.

Miss Kennett and her family have long accepted the former owner as one of their people. They are not overjoyed with her, but they understand why she is there. And if she looks out for them and the safety of their house—as Mary Wallace's ghost still does for the Ocean-born Mary House in Henniker, New Hampshire—then having Mrs. F. around isn't so bad after all!

Because the people involved in the following story are all prominent in present-day society in New England, I will not mention their names. Suffice it to say that I have them, and the story, to the best of my knowledge, is absolutely true.

Miss S. has a winter home on New York's East Side and a summer home in Massachusetts. All her life she had partaken of the supernatural, be it in little warnings or larger incursions from the so-called dead.

Once she was shopping at Bloomingdale's when she felt a sudden and inexplicable urge to visit her aged uncle in Washington Square. She tried to reason it out, saying to herself that the time of day was already too late for such a visit and that she should go the next morning, but the urge within her got the upper hand.

When she reached her uncle she found him happily smoking his pipe and in good spirits. He was an elderly gent and almost blind. Miss S. was sure that she had given in to a foolish impulse, but she went to take her coat off and hang it in the nurse's room. When she returned to her uncle, she saw that the bowl of his pipe had just caught fire and was blazing away, and he was not at all aware of it. Within moments, she managed to put out the fire. Had she not been there at the time, surely the uncle would have perished.

In 1940 Miss S. moved into her present summer home in Massachusetts. Seventeen years later she bought it from the friend who had owned it at the time. Built originally in 1904, the house had had a total of four owners prior to herself.

Her friend, a Mrs. R., had only owned the house for about a year when Miss S. moved in. Neither lady recalls anything unusual until one day in 1944, when they experienced something they could not explain by ordinary means. The house has a rear piazza in back of the living room, in direct line with the front door and the steps leading up to it. That day, they and some friends clearly heard some heavy footsteps coming up the front steps. Miss S. got up and hurried to see who it was, but found no one.

At first Miss S. dismissed it as some sort of practical joke, but she soon learned differently. Over the years, the steps would return, mainly in July and August, and always between noon and 3 P.M. Other phenomena included banging noises coming from an empty workshop once used by a former owner, and the clicking sound of a light switch being turned—but no light.

It became difficult to "explain" these happenings to the maid and various visitors, but Miss S. steadfastly refused to accept the supernatural explanation, although she knew at heart what it was.

Finally, the matter came to a head. Miss S. had been ill and her doctor was coming to see her. Since she was expecting him, she was sitting on the back piazza facing the front door. The doctor happened to be a cousin, and when she heard footsteps coming up the front steps she rose to greet him.

To her horror it was not her cousin who appeared now before her, but a strange man she had never seen before. He was a thin, elderly man in a Palm Beach suit and a panama hat.

Miss S. rushed to the door as fast as her feet would carry her, but he stepped sideways and just disappeared. She looked everywhere but there was no trace of the stranger. This experience so unnerved her she decided to discuss the apparition with her neighbors. It was then that she learned the story of her house. The man she had seen was indeed well know in the community. It was Mr. B., who had died in 1940. Up to 1939 the house had been owned by the P.'s, husband and wife. Mr. P. was an economist at one of the leading eastern universities. At the time, it was common knowledge in the community that a love affair had been going on between Mr. P. and Mrs. B., also dead now. The ghostly visitor was the husband, looking, apparently, for his wife at his neighbor's house.

What convinced Miss S. that this was indeed the case, was her friend's experience when she bought the house from the economist's wife. Overly anxious to sell the house, Mrs. P. took a sum below its actual value, and left everything in the house behind—even personal items such as the family Bible. Surely the house must have had bad memories for her and she wanted to get out as quickly as possible.

Well, Miss S. was not one bit amused. The prospect of having the ghost of the deceived husband dropping in on her unannounced did not please her at all. She took her Bible and said a few prayers in the firm New England manner that is part of her character. She followed this up with a request that Mr. B. should get his rest and not drop around again.

Either Mr. B. realized that the family scandal had better be forgotten now that he didn't have a ghost of a chance to do anything about his rival, or Miss S.'s direct approach worked.

Except for some tapping at her bedroom window in the summer of 1966, she did not hear any unusual noises again. And the tapping might have been *someone else*. After all, Miss S. is a receptive person.

14

THE ACCURSED FARMHOUSE

Enzersdorf on the river Fischa is a small hamlet of no great significance in the Austrian province of Lower Austria. The land around it is flat, the houses modest, and the streets dusty. Although the village is close enough to the capital for the more prosperous inhabitants to do their major shopping in Vienna, you get the feeling you're miles and miles from nowhere. That may be because this easternmost part of Austria had long been part of Hungary and the land had been owned by Hungarian noblemen, and their world is a quiet, slow-moving world in which modern progress has little significance. Some of the houses are very old and have stood here through Turkish occupations, French wars, and World Wars I and II, seemingly immune to the winds of change. One house in particular deserves notice: built of gray stone, of the kind that is quarried in the foothills of the Alps not too far away, it differs from the one-story farmhouses of the district in several ways: to begin with, it has a tile roof and very thick walls; only castles and fortresses have such walls in Austria. The outer wall encloses several buildings and the entire farmyard, thus making the house a world unto itself, as if it wanted to be safe from enemy attacks. Over the main gate, there is a coat of arms surmounted by an ecclesiastical design, for part of what is now an ordinary farmhouse was once a nunnery, although the name of it and the history of the order that built it are lost in antiquity. One family has owned the farmhouse for four centuries. Its ecclesiastical background goes back into the Middle Ages and one of the most turbulent periods in Austria's history.

The dusty road leading to the house is called the *Fischamenderstrasse*, the house bears the number 24, and despite its grimy gate, there is a surprisingly well-kept yard beyond the gate. To the left, as one enters, past a narrow stairway leading to a basement which I eventually got to know well indeed, one comes upon a sturdy, one-story farmhouse, the main living room of the Holler family. Next to it are the stables, followed further on by haylofts, another house, and the usual array of farm sheds and outbuildings, which line the other side of the yard, thus making the inner yard into an oblong within the stone walls. Evidently the building to the right of the gate had been the nunnery. But the phenomena that had brought me here were all concentrated in the left wing of the farm.

In 1964 a Vienna newspaper had seen fit to write about my activities in an uninformed and snide manner. A young farmer by the name of Rudolf Holler, Jr., had read the article and written to me asking for my help. Austria is not a land that takes kindly to psychic research. Strongly influenced by materialistic thought and yet still also under the remnants of clerical domination, Austrians as a whole don't like to mention such things as ghosts or psychic phenomena out of fear of being ridiculed. But this young man had a fine mind and his interests did include extrasensory perception. I was impressed by his plea and decided to go to Enzersdorf and see if I could break the ancient curse he felt was still operative at his ancestral farm.

Now curses are a strange thing. One's intellectual upbringing wants one to reject such a possibility, and yet the evidence exists: curses do work. For four centuries the family had been plagued by seemingly inexplicable misfortunes in its affairs. The presence of a restless spirit had been felt by many who had visited there, and ghostly manifestations had occurred. Above all, the animals were never well, no matter how healthy they had been before they were brought to the Holler stables. As soon as they were part of their farm, they became weak and showed unmistakable signs of disease. Cows would no longer give milk; horses turned lame; and even pigs, the sturdiest of domestic animals, lay listless and depressed, despite excellent feed and good treatment.

I was of course aware of ancient superstitions among farm folk concerning their livestock. Witchcraft accusations against innocent old women fill the annals of European history from the Middle Ages to the eighteenth century.

But Mr. Holler did not point the finger at any living person. He rationalized the facts as he saw them, and came to the conclusion that a wrong had been done to someone in the past, and that this wrong had never been righted. Thus the curse continued to be operative.

Nobody had ever tried to do anything about these conditions. The stories of the curse had been told from father to son until young Rudolf heard them as a child. But he was the first of the clan who knew what the word parapsychology meant. He was going to do something about the curse, and thus I found myself embarking on still another psychic adventure one summer day in 1965. Turhan Bey, my good friend and also a student of the occult, had offered to come along and drive my wife and me out to Enzersdorf.

We arrived in the late morning and immediately entered the farmhouse where Rudolf Holler and his family were already eagerly awaiting us. After I had looked around the place for a while, we settled down in the *gute Stube*, the good room, of the farmhouse and I asked Mr. Holler, the head of the family, to go over the problem with me.

"I myself have often heard knocks," he began, "always

between 7:30 and 8 P.M. There was no natural explanation." Finally the Hollers had brought in a douser. In an area where there was once a room, but which is today part of the stables, he discovered metal in the ground. He felt it signified buried coins.

For twenty-seven years, ever since he came to this house, Holler had heard the knocks. To him it sounded as if someone were lifting up a plate and smashing it down again against a table.

But the most frightening of the unusual phenomena in the Holler farmhouse goes back even beyond that time. A few years before, Holler's sister-in-law Maria Sladek was seated in the very room we were in now. Suddenly she saw an old woman with long, unkempt hair appear in the room, walking by the bed. Without taking any notice of her, the woman walked out through the closed door at the other end of the room—a door leading to the stables. She walked with a distinct limp, supporting herself with a cane. Mrs. Sladek was frozen with fear. She knew there was no such person at the farm at the time and moreover, in a small hamlet, everybody is known. But she had never seen this woman before in her life.

At first, she tried to pass the whole incident off as imaginary. But the stranger also appeared to an aunt and to a house guest who knew nothing whatever of the reputation of the farm as having a curse on it.

The curse showed itself in many ways. Holler had bought some of the finest cows in the district—cows that made him the envy of the area. But in a short while they turned ill and died.

"We tried to raise every kind of livestock in these stables," Holler explained. "Not only cows, but chickens, pigs, goats. They all died quickly. There was something in that spot that made it impossible for them to be well."

I shook my head. Perhaps there was some underground radiation?

But the ghostly visitation seemed to point in a different direction. Holler went to consult the local church records for the past four hundred years. No sign of any violence or murder. If any crime had been committed here, it hadn't left any traces. But Holler, who had married into the family that had owned the farm for so long, did notice one unusual fact: the previous owners, all the way back, had all died at early ages, disease was rampant among them, and the land belonging to the farm, instead of expanding in the course of time, became smaller and smaller until it reached the very modest size of today's farm. Evidently the place had been unlucky for four hundred years. I questioned Holler about the woman who walked through the wall. What did she look like?

"An old woman wearing old-fashioned clothes," he explained, "hair hanging down. Not of this period."

In the course of digging a cellar for an extension of the house, the Hollers came upon two human skeletons. The curious thing about these skeletons was an abundance of black spots in the area of the backbone, indicating that the two people had been poisoned. That was two years before our visit. It seemed to the Hollers that things quieted down after the discovery of the bones, but they did not wish to test their luck too much. Instead they moved into the newer portion of the farm. As for the accursed stables, they have been empty ever since. No sense exposing good animals to bad vibrations.

When the bones were discovered, the family held a council. What to do with them? It was decided to take the matter to the local parish priest. The good father listened quietly as the story of the discovery was unfolded before him.

"Look," he said at last, "this is a most unusual matter, most unusual. What shall we do about it?"

"Why, that's obvious, Reverend Father," Holler replied, "bury them in holy ground."

"That's just it," the priest countered. "How is the ground to remain truly holy, when all sorts of strange skeletons are being buried in it, I ask you?"

Holler was somewhat taken aback.

"But, Father," he began, "after all, these are people. People deserve to be buried in the cemetery."

"I know, I know," the priest said impatiently, walking up and down in his study, "but you see, we've had a couple suicides here lately, and it's been giving us a bad name. And now you come with God knows what sort of people."

"God knows," Holler said quietly.

"I tell you what," the priest said finally, as if he had stumbled upon the philosopher's stone, "here is what you do."

"Bring them over to you?"

"No, no, Heaven forbid, don't do that. Where exactly are they now—I mean the bones?"

"Where we found them, in the ground, down in the cellar."

"Good," the man of the cloth nodded, "in that case, leave them there."

"Leave them there? But Reverend Father, the trouble we've been having—the ghost—"

The priest threw him a stern, forbidding glance. Holler wished he hadn't mentioned the word.

"Leave them there," the priest intoned again, "just close up the hole and forget it."

Holler wasn't enthused by this suggestion, but he could not very well bury the skeletons in the cemetery without official permission.

He took his leave and went back to the farm. Then, with the help of his sons, he quietly closed the shallow grave in the cellar and hoped that it would be all right with the skeletons.

Unfortunately the trouble continued.

I decided to question Holler's wife now. Her maiden name intrigued me. She was born Anna Toifel, meaning Devil. It was her family that had owned this very house for five hundred years, and the house itself was five hundred years old. Not many farmhouses are.

In 1925 her grandparents saw the ghostly woman walk into the room. They noticed that her long, unkempt hair was gray.

"Nothing we touched in this house ever worked out," she explained, "from the animals, who died on us, to lost money and bad crops. It seems as if something or someone wants us to get out of the place."

"Do you actually feel a presence?"

"*Ja*, sometimes I feel there is someone in back of me."

"And is there?"

"No. I feel it all the way from here to the little house in the rear where we sleep now. Someone is at the door, the doorknob moves, and there is never anyone there. But I clearly heard the doorknob move."

Finally I turned to Rudolf Holler, Jr., age twenty-five, who had originally contacted me in New York. He is a trained locksmith and works as a driver for his father. When he was small, he used to sleep in a crib in the back room. Rarely did he have a peaceful night. Bad dreams kept waking him up. Over the years, these nightmares kept getting worse. Only six months before our visit, he woke up from a deep sleep around midnight. The outside gate had been opened, and footsteps resounded outside. The footsteps came up to the porch in front of the house, up the stairs to the bedroom. Rudolf, fully awake by that time, sat up in bed waiting for someone to open the door to his room. The handle was pressed down, as if a hand were on it, and then there was silence. No sound of retreating footsteps. Finally he jumped out of bed and opened the door. He was quite alone. It was just after 1 A.M. He then realized that the ghostly visitation had taken a full hour to cross the distance from the garden gate to his bedroom door, a distance he would walk in less than two minutes.

He never saw the "old woman with the long, gray hair" while he was awake, but she kept appearing in his dreams at frequent intervals, exactly as she had been described by his family.

I noticed that another young man had joined our little group. It turned out to be Engelbert, age eighteen, the younger son of the Hollers.

"Not long ago I went to the movies in the village," Engelbert reported, "and my mind was completely absorbed by the picture I had seen. When I returned home in the dark and reached the garden gate, I suddenly became aware of a white figure standing near it. In a moment it was gone."

"What did it look like?"

"It was a luminous figure, thin and high—you couldn't make out any features or anything."

The bed stood over the spot where the skeletons had been found farther down. After the discovery of the bones, the restless nights ceased.

There matters stood at present, and the Hollers had the uneasy feeling that the curse was far from lifted. The bones were still not in hallowed ground. At first Mrs. Holler had objected to leaving them where they had been found. The priest wouldn't budge in his opposition to giving the skeletons a "Christian burial."

"Bury 'em in the garden," he finally advised Mrs. Holler. But that wouldn't do, either. The garden was no more appropriate than the cellar. So they had remained down there, and we decided to have a look at the spot.

There, barely visible in the murky semidarkness of the cellar, was nothing more than a stone slab in a cellar wall. Hardly a suitable grave. The Hollers had come with me and stood around now, waiting for some action. I did not have a medium with me so I had to try and get through to the retless ones myself. Turhan Bey seemed depressed by the mere thought of the violence that had caused these unknown people's deaths.

Quickly I said a quiet prayer for them, asking them not to hold the present owners of the house responsible for whatever ancient wrongs might have been done to them.

Then we returned to the sunlight. It was about two o'clock by now and the Hollers brought out some country wine to share with us.

Afterwards, we toured the rest of the farm and then wished them good-bye.

On Easter of 1966, I heard again from Rudolf Holler, Jr. Things were still very tricky at the farm. The two boys had been standing in the entrance recently, working on a car. Rudolf was standing exactly above the spot where the two skeletons were still buried. The time was 2:30 P.M. and it was a quiet, chilly March day. Suddenly a strong gust of wind tore open the gate to the road, enveloped Rudolf in a blast of chilly air, and rushed on to close the inner gate with a loud bang. The two young men looked at each other in bewilderment. There had been no wind, no draft, nothing that could have caused so violent a reaction.

But shortly afterwards, one of their two valued geese, a breeding animal, became unaccountably ill and had to be killed.

Rudolf asked that I return to Enzersdorf with a trance medium, realizing that the restless one had not yet found peace.

I have not heard further from the Hollers. Either they have adjusted to living in an accursed house, or the old lady with the cane has recognized her true status, perhaps stirred up by my ceremonial service at the "grave" of the two skeletons.

Were these her victims? Was she earthbound because of what she had done?

Poisoning of humans as well as animals was a favorite way of bringing destruction to one's enemies in the sixteenth century. Were we dealing here with a rural Lucrezia Borgia?

I can't help thinking that the village priest should have accepted the two skeletons among his dead flock. Being buried close to a former nunnery isn't the same thing. Only the consecrated ground of a regular graveyard will do. That is, if you're a discriminating skeleton.

EPILOGUE

The work of the Psychic Investigator is never done. Nor is it dull. My files keep expanding, my correspondence gets heavier and heavier, just as the limbs of my hypnotized subjects when I do psychotherapy with them.

The tools of my trade are mainly in my head—to appraise the reports and facts as they present themselves, to draw certain conclusions from them and to do something about it—or not—as the case may be.

Not every case coming in is genuine in psychic terms. The world harbors a goodly number of unbalanced people as well as a very large number of healthy individuals with strange experiences in their lives. Only long years of work in this field coupled with a certain native intelligence and a keen, open-minded judgment can give one the ability to tell the true from the false. But so much authentic material has turned up and is continuously coming into view, that only the uninformed or grossly prejudiced individual would deny the validity of this field of inquiry. Final conclusions may not be possible in certain areas of this work, but strong views may nevertheless be held by those at the epicenter of the evidence, and it is not only their privilege, but their duty to make these views known to others and to carefully report on their findings. Facts are not subject to dismissal by those who did not find the facts or were not present when someone else found them. They are subject to different personal interpretation, of course, but the validity of conclusions drawn by outsiders with hindsight seems to me a lot weaker than the fresh and carefully weighed impressions and views of the researcher on the spot.

It amazes me that psychic research, which deals with man's true nature and is certainly a vitally important endeavor, should have to continually defend itself from accusations by the unqualified and biased, while equally recent sciences, such as space research or advanced electronics, are highly honored occupations at liberty to promulgate the unproven, the hoped for, the tentative, at will—and be praised for being so progressive.

Is it perhaps because man's soul is involved when we deal with the evidence presenting proof of individual survival of death? Do we shy away from coming to grips with ultimate truth concerning our true nature, because somehow deep within us we fear that truth? Because knowledge of this great truth does not make us free—on the contrary, it makes us bound, bound to the intangible ties of morality and self-esteem. How many among us are truly satisfied with their lives? How many are proud of all they have done, thought, believed, and said through the years of their lives?

Now a science, a hard-core method of proof, comes along and tells them that the grave is not the end. That all their thoughts, actions, and feelings continue on into the next state of being.

This requires a complete overhauling of their customary philosophy of life, for if the essential part of man's personality survives physical death, any existence ignoring this future life is, at the very best, partial, at the worst, clouded with misconceptions and errors.

Few people are prepared to chuck their comfortable materialistic point of view in favor of a wider spiritual frontier.

Those who do have found that their lives suddenly take on dramatic new meaning, and they are no longer part of a senseless patchwork, but links in a great, orderly universe, playing their roles properly, and finding life always rewarding, no matter what their circumstances might be.

Knowledge does not make you free, but it makes you free to choose.

Those desiring to contact me may do so, whether to report a psychic experience or seeking help, provided they write legibly or, even better, type their message or query, and attach a stamped, self-addressed envelope with it. The mailing address is: Hans Holzer, 140 Riverside Drive, New York, N.Y. 10024.

Vale!